Jeremy S Brumbelow

Historical
Thought
in America

UNIVERSITY OF OKLAHOMA PRESS : NORMAN

Timothy Paul Donovan

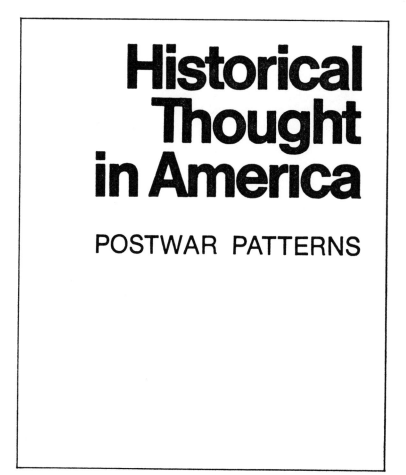

Historical Thought in America

POSTWAR PATTERNS

The paper on which this book is printed bears the watermark of the University of Oklahoma Press and has an effective life of at least three hundred years.

By Timothy Paul Donovan

Henry Adams and Brooks Adams: The Education of Two American Historians (Norman, 1961)
Historical Thought in America: Postwar Patterns (Norman, 1973)

Library of Congress Cataloging in Publication Data

Donovan, Timothy Paul.
 Historical thought in America: postwar patterns.
 Bibliography: p.
 1. Historiography—History.   2. Historians—United States.
  I.   Title
D13.D63   907'.2'073   72–9272

to
Kevin,
Becky,
David,
Ricky,
and their mother

Preface

The atomic weapons which brought an end to World War II also were the signals for reassessment of principles and values in most areas of American life. Historical thought was no exception. Historians in America since 1945 have undertaken a re-examination of themselves and their craft which clearly demonstrates that the war was both a watershed and a catalyst. This book attempts to explain the pattern of this postwar introspection and to delineate those particular trends which seem most significant for the future. While this study concerns itself only with the ideas of historians, it is my contention that historical thought transcends disciplinary limitations and is an important facet of general intellectual history—a barometer of the times as well as intramural dialogue.

Many historians have been considered, practically all who have written on the subject. Nor was the research confined solely to writers of American history; it included any historian in America, whatever his particular field of interest. Examination, however, has not been extended to the professional philosopher. The qualifying mark has been that of the working historian.

The dominant thrust of postwar historical thought has been toward a revitalized humanism, but a humanism which seeks to maintain the standards of scientific history. In thinking about such basic historical problems as the role of the individual, the mechanics of causality and the proper sphere of metahistory, historians have generally sought to re-emphasize the significance of personality and human values in the drama of history. At least these are the ideas which I have found significant and attractive. There is, therefore, a point of view expressed, as well as a survey of postwar historical thought in America.

Many of my colleagues and students have shown remarkable forbearance during the years that this book was in preparation. Over many cups of coffee fellow historians have listened to my ideas, discussed and debated them at length, and given me the benefits of their insight and understanding. My students through their capacity to ask questions I found difficult to answer were a constant stimulus to the project. However, I am especially indebted to Professors James V. Reese, of Texas Tech University; John S. Ezell, of the University of Oklahoma; Donald F. Whisenhunt, of Thiel College; and Gordon H. McNeil, of the University of Arkansas, each of whom read and criticized the entire manuscript. Their suggestions were most helpful even when their advice was not followed. The responsibility, certainly, for errors in either style or substance is mine alone. I am also grateful to Texas Tech University for two summer research grants which greatly facilitated my work.

My wife, Eugenia Trapp Donovan, merits more than the usual commendation. In addition to typing the manuscript she was equally proficient as literary critic and morale builder. Without her steadfastness and encouragement the project would not have been completed.

TIMOTHY P. DONOVAN

January 15, 1973
Fayetteville, Arkansas

Contents

Preface   *page* vii

CHAPTER 1   Introduction   3

2   Historians, History, and the World Crisis   16

3   The Historical Function   32

4   The Individual Among Historians   56

5   Causality: Continuity and Contingency   75

6   History and Metahistory   98

7   The Perfect Historian   112

8   Redefining History   131

Bibliography   147

Index   179

**Historical
Thought
in America**

The world of comfortable assumptions disappeared forever with the mushroom-shaped clouds that hovered briefly over the ruins of Hiroshima and Nagasaki. Not only did the second international holocaust of the twentieth century terminate with an abrupt and terrible finality, but also concluded was humanity's most basic presupposition: the permanence of life itself.

That older and safer world had been tottering for two generations under a series of savage shocks which were all the more devastating for their being unforeseen. The wholesale slaughter in the trenches of World War I had demonstrated clearly that "civilized" nations, like the individuals of which they were composed, were often trapped by tragic circumstances and their own proneness to irrationality. And having barely recovered from what had been hoped was the temporary insanity of 1914 to 1918, Western civilization was forced to witness the fashioning of a fascist mystique which extolled the darker side of human nature, made organized murder the official policy of the state, and mocked society's pretensions to progress and reason. Yet the inferno created by the release of the power of the atom was more than just the finishing horror of the nightmare; it was also the beginning of the quest for new guidelines now that the older validities seemed to be gone. The result was a spiritual and intellectual chaos from which we have not yet emerged. History and historians shared the dilemma of philosophers, theologians, and scientists. For the first time history itself confronted oblivion.

In the light of such ultimate uncertainty the age since 1945 has been a time of intense questioning of traditional values, and ofttimes the failure to achieve any surety has resulted in despair. Deprived of ancient rudders, the man of the atomic era has desperately sought

3

new formulas with which he might fathom a universe grown increasingly complex. The result has been ferment and change in almost every field of human thought and aspiration. The sciences, the arts, the humanities, the social sciences, philosophy, and religion all have undergone reanalysis, reinterpretation to meet the demand for new knowledge, new guidelines, and, above all, new hope. However dispassionate the scholar, he is also aware that any convulsive holocaust will destroy his ivory tower, as well as the civilization of which it is a part. Consequently, one discerns a sense of urgency in the quest for meaning in even the most prosaic of disciplines, and in those areas of thought and study where man has attempted to understand man the time for leisurely perusal is over. Time, once believed virtually limitless, has been found to have the individual man's great burden, finiteness.

New solutions and approaches have been as varied as there have been searchers. To many in philosophy the modern expression of existentialism found in Jean-Paul Sartre or Albert Camus has seemed especially attractive because of its emphasis upon the here and now as opposed to either the hitherto or the hereafter. To others philosophy had lost its capacity for larger meaning and was limited to attempting semantic precision. Sociologists, psychologists, and political scientists have succumbed with increasing frequency to the blandishments of behaviorism. Replete with models, graphs, and charts, these social scientists have comforted themselves with the thought that some certainty about a narrow and confined area of study is preferable to the remoter possibilities for establishing any kind of truth in work of a broader scope. Theologians and religious thinkers have offered the alternatives of a return to faith through the neo-orthodoxy of Karl Barth, Paul Tillich, and Reinhold Niebuhr or a rejection of theism in the "God is dead" school. The graphic and musical arts have been characterized by the retreat of the individual artist into the world of self as the only possible avenue of understanding, while literature has undergone a similar transformation. The theater of the absurd, the cacophony of modern orchestration, poetic preoccupation with meaningless sound, and the popular penchant for pop art illustrate the failure of the individual to discover social significance in the world outside himself.

This book is concerned with what the historian in America has done. Has he attempted any redefinition of his discipline? Has he interpreted the anxiety of the new age as affecting his craft? The answer is yes to both questions. There has been a real soul searching about the very nature of his mission. While in England this intramural dialogue has received wide currency through the public disputations of E. H. Carr, Arnold J. Toynbee, and others, in the United States the trend has been for such discussion to be undertaken beneath the surface. But before that self-analysis can be examined, it is necessary to establish its relevance.

Historians have long been concerned with ideas and their impact on human history. Even a casual reading of any great historian will confirm this observation. Thucydides wrote not only of the military activities of the Peloponnesian War but also of the intellectual configurations which produced an Athens and a Sparta. Francis Parkman, while eloquently describing the Anglo-French confrontation in the North American wilderness, also sought to expose and explain those ideas and customs which had created two such divergent cultures. Indeed, historians have demonstrated as consistent an interest in the why of history as in the what and the how. It has only been in the last generation, however, that intellectual history has acquired an identity and scope of its own.[1] The frustrations and problems have been many, the debates over function and definition have been vigorous; but few would today deny either the reality or the relevance of the subject to the historiographical scene.

At first glance the term "intellectual history" seems easily capable of definition. What could be more natural and objective than to describe it as simply the history of ideas? But such a simplistic definition, attractive as it may be in its succinctness, makes no discrimi-

---

[1] Convenient dates to mark the emergence of intellectual history as an organized discipline in the United States might well be 1936, with the publication of Arthur Lovejoy's *Great Chain of Being*; and 1940, with the founding of the *Journal of the History of Ideas*. It should be emphasized that the study of the history of ideas is by no means a contemporary development for either European or American historians. I am speaking here only of its status as a systematized branch of history.

nation about *what* ideas are proper material for the historian's scrutiny. Should the historian bother only with those ideas significant to philosophic, literary, or scientific thought, or should he be concerned with all ideas which have some impact upon the popular mind and culture? The question is crucial, for, as Rush Welter has recently observed, "a discipline is defined at least as much by the questions it does not seek to answer as by those it does."[2] Consequently, historians of ideas have felt compelled to refine their definitions, to delineate their areas of responsibility, and to determine their proper focus of attention. This winnowing process has produced some consensus although by no means unanimity.

The opinion which has gained the widest acceptance is that intellectual history must attempt through its researches the illumination of a given historical era or age. Specifically, it must show how and in what ways the prevailing concepts of one epoch are different from those of both preceding and succeeding periods of time. Conversely, it must not become so enamored of that which is new that it forgets or ignores the familiar and the constant. Yet intellectual history, like all branches of Clio's muse, must emphasize and explain singularity. As a result the center of research must concentrate upon the hinge of change, for it is the times of transition that most clearly disclose what have been the controlling presuppositions or ideas of the age then ending. J. H. Randall, Jr., claims as the function of intellectual history "the reasons for changes in standards and principles," and John C. Greene believes that one of the primary goals of the intellectual historian is to explain the alterations which ideas "undergo from epoch to epoch."[3] By emphasizing the changes which occur, the historian is then freed to recreate the *Zeitgeist* of that period he has selected for study.

In seeking the ideological unity of an age, the intellectual historian acts upon an implicit assumption of faith: that the nature of society

[2] Rush Welter, "The History of Ideas in America: An Essay in Redefinition," *Journal of American History*, Vol. LI (March, 1965), 599.

[3] J. H. Randall, Jr., review of John U. Nef, *The United States and Civilization*, in *American Historical Review*, Vol. XLVIII (January, 1943), 345; John C. Greene, "Objectives and Methods in Intellectual History," *Mississippi Valley Historical Review*, Vol. XLIV (June, 1957), 59.

is to be found in its ideas. Carried further, this thesis implies that such ideas are the basic determinants of other historical events. If the hypothesis and its corollary are true, the intellectual historian has come to the heart of societal experience.

To reveal the fabric of an era's experience through its ideas is, however, a task of great complexity; it is also one beset by frustration and pitfall. Both understanding and wide-ranging knowledge are obvious prerequisites. The historian must not only know traditional history but also be alert to developments, techniques, and trends within a variety of disciplines not ordinarily deemed the province of the historian. Leonard Krieger points out that such competence is essential if the historian is to "distinguish between what occurs as an insulated response to such technical issues and what occurs as an open response to the more general influences of the era."[4] If it is literature with which he is dealing, he must not allow the interesting anecdote, the stylistic variation, or the preoccupation with literary trivia to obscure the relationship between the writing of an age and its larger themes. Yet the historian must be familiar enough with the meaningful and the ephemeral of the literature of a period to make the necessary distinction.

Another temptation which must be resisted is the inclination to dehumanize ideas, to divorce thought from its human progenitors. It is all too easy to do, for ideas, especially those of influence and vitality, seem often to possess lives of their own. Moreover, the Procrustean impulse is strong in all of us, and the desire to categorize, to fit things into convenient niches is frequently overwhelming. Ideas devoid of the human passions which produced them are more easily pigeonholed. The intellectual historian, like all historians, must keep in mind that his focus should be on the individual. Arthur O. Lovejoy, a pioneer in the field, put it simply and forcefully: "the actor in the piece, its hero—some would in these days say, its villain—is still homo sapiens."[5]

---

[4] Leonard Krieger, "The Horizons of History," *American Historical Review*, Vol. LXIII (October, 1957), 67.

[5] Arthur O. Lovejoy, "Reflections on the History of Ideas," *Journal of the History of Ideas*, Vol. I (January, 1940), 8. Lovejoy goes on to say that the "general task

The intellectual historian may also find himself trapped by his preoccupation with the rationality of ideas. After all, that is what he generally seeks to find in his studies. Thus the discovery of the operation of irrationality within the historical process can be exceedingly frustrating. The first thought is to discard the discovery or at the very least to ignore it. Yielding to that desire may simplify the historian's task and obviate the difficulty of a complicated answer to a straightforward question, but it will do so at the risk of distortion and dishonesty. Man is governed by the illogical as well as the logical. Not all the ideas and beliefs he holds are the products of rational thought, and the historian of ideas must be prepared to confront the paradox of man's growing control over natural forces "made ridiculous by the powerful impact of irrationality in the twentieth century in such forms as the demoniacal Hitler or the continued existence of racial prejudice."[6]

A plethora of material may be as much of a problem for the historian of ideas as his quest for rationality in human thought. The cultural records for practically any period are so numerous as to defy their total assimilation by a single researcher. Selectivity becomes, therefore, an almost automatic function, as it is for all historians; but for the intellectual historian discrimination in his selection process is vital. Such picking and choosing must be conducted with an eye toward not only what is artistic and sensitive but also what is revealing and expository. This is especially true when dealing with the literature of a period, but the same caution should be applied to other areas. The ordinary sampling techniques so often employed by the political or economic historian cannot be employed with similar assurance by the intellectual historian. As Louis Filler reminds us, to treat the fiction of William Allen White on the same level as that of Theodore Dreiser "is to miss much of the intellectual history of the past fifty years."[7]

---

of intellectual historiography is to exhibit so far as may be, the thinking animal engaged . . . in his most characteristic occupation."

[6] Richard E. Sullivan, "Toynbee's Debtors," *South Atlantic Quarterly*, Vol. LVIII (Winter, 1959), 81.

[7] Louis Filler, review of Perry Miller (ed.), *The Transcendentalists: An Anthology*, in *American Historical Review*, Vol. LVI (October, 1950), 131–32.

Eventually, having avoided as many of the aforementioned dangers as he possibly can, the historian of thought must be prepared to allow his intuition to be a final, but necessary, catalyst in revealing the inner dynamic of an age. At some point in his research the period will begin to appear to him in its totality, and he will see both its unifying characteristics and its paradoxes, its relationship to times past and its pertinence to the future. He will discover that central to his study is "the search for connections between bodies of thought and related areas of intellectual or social experience."[8] Matters hitherto believed extraneous or insignificant will be seen as part of the fabric he is attempting to reveal. No historian's achievement is more personally rewarding or more professionally valuable. Certainly the historian can aspire to no higher goal than to provide his readers and hearers with an insight into the core of the historical process: the formation of a web of ideas so interwoven within the context of time and space that individual threads become indistinguishable in the network of both rich color and softer nuance. A part of that portrait of an age is its historiography—and a not-unimportant part.

It has become a cliché to assert that each age rewrites history for its own use and in light of its own experience. No historian today would seriously question the conventional wisdom of this statement or its complementary declaration that the individual historian brings to his task the virtues and deficiencies, the enlightenment and prejudice, and the liberating and restricting experiences of his own life and his own time. Historiography at any particular moment in time is a reflection, to a greater or lesser degree, of the age in which it was written. Historians, consequently, become not only the chroniclers of the past but also indicators of the currents of their own time. Frequently they are more than mere passive direction pointers; at crisis points they often become active forces in molding and shaping the intellectual environment in which they live.[9] When this occurs, as it decidedly has since 1945 in the United States, historical thought

[8] John Higham, "The Rise of American Intellectual History," *American Historical Review*, Vol. LVI (April, 1951), 453.

[9] Wallace K. Ferguson, *The Renaissance in Historical Thought*, 387.

takes its place alongside other forms of intellectual endeavor as a basic part of intellectual history and as such merits study from that broader vantage point. What historians have to say about the nature, method, and substance of their craft in such situations should have more than parochial interest; it should aid in understanding the quality and texture of the era of which they are a part.

Just as the development of self-consciousness marked the emergence of man from savagery and separated him forever from the world of his fellow mammals, so the refinement of a sharp historiographical sense was the necessary concomitant to the maturation of society as a whole and to its historians in particular. The ability to understand the collective past, to reflect on otherwise forgotten accounts of that past, and to evaluate critically the record keepers was fundamental in maintaining a civilized perspective and, at the same time, an essential facet of self-knowledge. By studying the history of history, historians could see themselves in their previous incarnations as products of a special time and place; it was a necessary humiliation, for only with such analysis could better history be written. Only by comparing points of view from the present to the past and back again could the shape of contemporary bias and prejudice be revealed. What was observed in the writings of earlier practitioners could often be applied to later ones. Consequently, the study of historiography became for the historian one of the mechanisms by which he might gain insight not just into the methodology of his own craft but into its substance as well. In short, historiography makes the historian aware that he, as a writer and teacher of history, is also part of history.[10]

The historians writing in the postwar era have undertaken as comprehensive a self-analysis as those analyses which accompanied the transition from literary to scientific historiography or the subsequent challenge of the relativists to the objectivists. Hundreds of articles and a significant quantity of books testify to the ferment.

[10] Peter Gay, *A Loss of Mastery*, 20; Roland H. Bainton, "Interpretations of the Reformation," *American Historical Review*, Vol. LXVI (October, 1960), 74; Louis Gottschalk, "A Professor of History in a Quandary," *American Historical Review*, Vol. LIX (January, 1954), 285.

Whether such activity signals another new direction for historians remains to be seen, but certainly such intense introspection cannot help but result in some measure of reorientation and a refocusing of attention on some areas neglected or overlooked by previous writers. Generally, historians seem to be concerned with those matters which relate directly to the role of the individual within the historical process. There is increasing anxiety about the role of the personality in a world seemingly ever more dominated by impersonal forces.[11] Committed to man as the central theme of history, historians have found it difficult to diminish his importance without demeaning their own. Other topics which have been seriously scrutinized are those dealing with definitions of history, the functions of history and the historian, the relative values of historical-mindedness and present-mindedness, the role of contingency in historical causation and causation itself, the whole matter of interpretation in history, and the virtue or lack of it in the pursuit of metahistory. Subsequent chapters will explore the impact which a professional re-examination has had on these crucial areas of historical concern.

As the barriers against modern barbarism crumbled for the second time in a quarter of a century when Hitler's armies stormed across the Polish frontier in 1939, historians in the United States found themselves singularly unprepared to afford an anxious public either solace or understanding. This is not to say that members of the guild had ceased to practice their craft but rather that, since the termination of the first global conflict in 1918, they had been made more cautious in their research and more restrained in their desire to generalize. This timidity derived partly from the naturally conservative canons of historical methodology and partly from the experiences and battles of the interwar years. The image of the historian as objective interpreter of the past had also been tarnished by his partisan involvement in the propaganda activities of 1917 to 1919. In light of the many revisionist works concerning relative war guilt

11 One writer has explained the concern this way: "If a study of the historiography of any period is a fairly reliable barometer of the concerns of the period itself, it may be concluded that our own age asks analytical questions about its past primarily because it is terribly upset about itself." R. H. Bastert, "The New American History and Its Audience," *Yale Review*, Vol. XLVI (December, 1956), 249.

and the reasons for American entry into the war which enjoyed wide circulation in the twenties and thirties, the reading public could well ask embarrassing questions concerning the validity of any claim to impartiality by the professional as well as the amateur historian.[12] A goodly portion of the blame for this lack of credibility can be assessed to those who claimed for history a scientism it did not inherently possess. Page Smith, in his provocative *The Historian and History*, ably summarizes the dilemma:

> The problems would have been simple enough if, with the destruction of traditional society, historians had indeed been what they claimed to be—the objective interpreters of the past. Had they, by some alchemy, been able to stand outside time, they could presumably, have identified the hideous deformities which were to be the shame of the twentieth century and thus made possible the creation of a future free of them. But they could not, and their pose of objectivity in most instances simply made them more vulnerable to the grosser prejudices of their time and their nation.[13]

Indeed, within professional ranks the relativist attacks upon the truisms of "scientific history" had created divisions that added to the reluctance of historians to commit themselves to schemes of broad interpretation or the ascription of meaning to the events of the past.

Unlike his predecessors of the Progressive period the historian in the United States on the eve of World War II affected a detachment from the tumultuous events swirling around him. Nor did he regard his historical studies with the same passion evidenced by a John Bassett, a William Dodd, or a Vernon Parrington. Charles G. Sellers suggests that in the case of interpreters of Jacksonian democracy this detachment was due to the more urban orientation of historians who came of age during the New Deal and whose "stance seems to be that of self-conscious intellectuals . . . expressing through their detached . . . analysis an alienation from the middle-class mainstream of

12 For an excellent study of the writings of the revisionists and their influence see Warren I. Cohen, *The American Revisionists: The Lessons of Intervention in World War I.*

13 Page Smith, *The Historian and History*, 60.

American life that is reminiscent of the patrician school." Whatever the cause, the attitude was certainly pervasive; moreover, it was much safer to remain uncommitted to any philosophical system or set of values which might compromise the historian's claim to objectivity. Yet, in itself, this posture of the scientist had been undermined by the aforementioned assaults of the relativists so that, at best, historians seemed to take refuge in what H. Stuart Hughes has described as a sort of "truncated positivism."[14] This rejection of responsibility was seriously challenged by the holocaust of war with its attendant human miseries and nuclear dilemma. From within the profession the appearance of Arnold Toynbee's *A Study of History* in its popular abridgment also questioned the validity of an approach to history which did not take as its goal both synthetic and ultimate meaning, and, finally, academic historians in the United States began to rethink some of the basic presuppositions which most had found so comfortable only a few years before.

A fundamental reason why the historian found it impossible to escape the concerns of the world around him was the very nature of Western society. Western man understands himself and his environment in terms of their history. He is incapable of discovering significance in any other way owing in part to the eschatology of Christianity and also to his devotion to the idea of progress which, in many different guises, has remained a constant. Indeed, "history, process, change, are notions hardly distinguishable from each other in Western conceptualization."[15] The rise of German historicism in the nineteenth century and its infiltration into the bedrock of American thought were additional contributing factors. At any rate it was only natural that a society so dedicated to viewing itself from a historical and evolutionary point of view should come to demand that its historians be more than mere record keepers or fussy antiquarians who emerged from their studies periodically to deliver

14 Charles G. Sellers, "Andrew Jackson Versus the Historians," *Mississippi Valley Historical Review*, Vol. XLIV (March, 1958), 631; H. Stuart Hughes, "The Historian and the Social Scientist," *American Historical Review*, Vol. LXVI (October, 1960), 24–25.

15 J. J. Finkelstein, "Mesopotamian Historiography," American Philosophical Society *Proceedings*, Vol. CVII (1963), 461.

luncheon talks to local genealogical groups. Society demanded a workable relevant history which attempted to make some sense out of the bewildering proliferation of problems and crises which characterized the twentieth century.

In January, 1946, Professor Carlton J. H. Hayes, recently returned from a wartime ambassadorial assignment in Spain, argued that one of the most conspicuous failings of American historiography was its parochialism, its "tendency to turn away from European themes." Declaring that the past seventy years of historical scholarship in America had constituted another self-imposed Babylonian Captivity, Hayes urged his fellow workers to devote more time to non-American history. True, there had already been some progress in this direction since 1917, and the introduction of the Western civilization course in many college curricula was the best example of broadening interest in hitherto esoteric areas.[16] Yet there was still an obvious deficiency in this regard.

Looking at the state of American historiography from the reverse side of the lens, Roy F. Nichols maintained that the microcosm of local history had likewise been ignored. Comparing the research and writing of history at the community level to atomic exploration, the University of Pennsylvania scholar urged the use of sampling techniques and other devices to explore those areas "where social forces germinate." In advocating methods long practiced by the historian's co-workers in the social sciences, Nichols struck a most sensitive nerve, for the argument whether history could properly employ the techniques of the sociologist or the political scientist had long been debated. Richard Hofstadter, himself a pioneer in the use of such concepts, declared in 1950 that American historians were still ignoring the methodological avenues "opened by Beard thirty-seven years ago."[17] The matter still remains one of considerable heat, for if anything has characterized the re-examination of the generation

[16] Carlton J. H. Hayes, "The American Frontier—Frontier of What?" *American Historical Review*, Vol. LI (January, 1946), 202; John Higham *et al.*, *History*, 42.

[17] Roy F. Nichols, "Postwar Reorientation of Historical Thinking," *American Historical Review*, Vol. LIV (October, 1948), 80. Richard Hofstadter, "Beard and the Constitution: The History of an Idea," *American Quarterly*, Vol. II (Fall, 1950), 204.

since 1945, it has been a concern with the function and scope of historians and history.

Despite these and other areas of dissatisfaction with the state of historical writing at the onset of the postwar period, the bulk of published writing has remained largely within a traditional and conservative framework. A. S. Eisenstadt observed as late as 1963 that the four major historiographical currents were continued reliance upon the narrative form, a persistent presentation of political themes, a cult of biography used in conventional ways, and the release of meticulously edited compilations of the papers of the Founding Fathers.[18] This seeming surface traditionalism did not, however, adequately reflect the ferment of ideas that were boiling from below and has resulted in a much more severe analysis, which, in time, may well produce a revolution in the writing of history in America.

The larger challenge facing the American historian is one which has humanistic and philosophical as well as historical connotations. It recognizes that the historian cannot divorce himself from the concerns of his time and that he cannot divest himself of the responsibility which is implicit within his function. To believe that his work is meaningful implies a responsibility to convey its significance to his hearers and readers. To believe that his labors are without import reduces him to the role of dilettante at best and social parasite at worst. The historian as individual human being and the historian as scholar are not separate components which can be arbitrarily compartmentalized. Any thinking man has to be too existentially involved to allow himself the luxury of daily excursions into Olympian aloofness. The historian has to ask what relationship exists between the practice of historianship and the destiny of the world of which he is a part. He can but hope that his search for self-understanding will illuminate for society some of the places it has been and disclose its options for the future.

---

[18] A. S. Eisenstadt, "American History and Social Science," in A. S. Eisenstadt (ed.), *The Craft of American History*, II, 115–16.

CHAPTER 2

**Historians,
History,
and the World Crisis**

World War II dramatized as nothing else could have the apocalyptic
nature of modern society and awakened historians and others to
the general cultural crisis of the twentieth century. The war "inspired
a crisis literature that lumped the pasts of all segments of Western
civilization together into common transmission of society toward the
present."[1] But the war, with the implicit threat of extinction produced by the feat of atomic fission, was really a culmination rather
than a beginning. If by 1945 man's physical presence on the earth
was in jeopardy, his spiritual stability had been steadily eroded since
the advent of industrialized society and mass technology. The dark
forebodings entertained by Henry Adams at the World's Columbian
Exposition in 1893 concerning the dynamo and its impact upon the
direction of civilization had been truly prophetic. What T. S. Eliot
had described in *The Wasteland*, what Edward Arlington Robinson
had observed in the people of *Tilbury Town*, what innumerable
artists, poets, and philosophers had said in many and various ways
were now recognized as insightful and predictive. All had pointed
to the dehumanization which had seemed inherent in the progress of
technology. Not only was man at the mercy of a universe discovered
to be ever more vast and impersonal but also he was seemingly
unable to control those forces which he himself had created and
unleashed. Impotence increased the frustration.

Often obscured in the resulting confusion was the fact that the
crisis was a total one. It was impossible to separate into discrete
elements the matter of physical survival and spiritual decay. Just as
the individual human being is an integrated whole who must be
considered a combination of the corporeal and the psychic, so must

[1] Leonard Krieger in Higham *et al.*, *History*, 289.

the modern maladies affecting the human condition be treated in their entirety. It would do no good to attempt a cure which ignored either aspect of the problem. Moreover, the dual nature of the dilemma was complicated and enlarged by its general historical nature, which was comparable in its dimensions, Thomas S. Harrison maintains, to the fall of Rome, the transition from the medieval to the modern mind, and "to the powerful upheaval wrought by the French Revolution at the end of the eighteenth century."[2] Since the crisis was not just that of the individual but was in addition national, even global, in character, it became susceptible to historical explanation if not solution. The historian, then, had to assume some responsibility toward comprehension, and with the onset of World War II a few historians began to acknowledge the obligation.

As early as 1940, in the first issue of the *Journal of the History of Ideas*, Arthur O. Lovejoy anticipated the question which so many historians would ask in forthcoming years by declaring that the central problem of the time was that of human nature. Pointing the way to a new emphasis upon humane studies, Lovejoy maintained that "the question which more than any other demands answer is the question, 'What's the matter with man?' "[3] Many, of course, believed that they already had the answer, especially those who were religiously oriented. Man's salvation must come from the recapturing of the traditional spiritual values which the onrush of technological and material advance had caused to be forgotten. The crisis of world war afforded a rich opportunity for such a renewal inasmuch as people were searching for anchorage in a world in which safe harbors seemed to have disappeared. Admitting that history because of its close scrutiny of the past might well offer clues to the understanding and solution of present problems, Hugh S. Tigner insisted that only by adopting a moral view of the historical process could historians meet popular needs for some surety.[4] Not many professional his-

[2] Thomas S. Harrison, "The Historian and Crisis," *Prairie Schooner*, Vol. XXV (1951), 167–68.

[3] Lovejoy, Reflections on the History of Ideas," *Journal of the History of Ideas*, Vol. I (January, 1940), 8–9.

[4] Hugh S. Tigner, "The Religious View of History," *Christian Century*, Vol. LVIII (May 21, 1941), 682–84.

torians, to be sure, were ready to discard scientific objectivity and return to the practice of substituting moral dogmatics for scholarship, but many were alarmed by the popular acclaim given to historical prophets like Oswald Spengler and H. G. Wells.

Spengler, whose pessimistic predictions about the future of Western society attracted many alienated intellectuals in the interim between the wars, enjoyed a revival of interest at the popular level with the advent of World War II. Some writers interpreted this development as evidence of the world's need for meaningful answers to contemporary experience and warned that professional historians were in danger of having their labors ignored by a reading audience who preferred metahistorical schemes to the tedium of conventional historical investigation so often pedestrian in its literary craftsmanship and unwilling to extract meaning from its researches.[5] Obviously, historians had to become in some manner more flexible in their outlook; perspective needed to be enlarged. World War I had "led a number of people outside the academies to undertake an anxious examination of the past."[6] World War II forced the academicians to do the same thing.

Most agreed that the crucial question which now confronted the historian was the knotty and often neglected problem of historical causation. It was evident that simple narrative or descriptive history would no longer suffice in discharging the historian's obligation. He must go further in explaining how the mysterious wellsprings of the past had led to the turbulent present. Unless he grappled with this most ancient of historical problems, he might well discover that the contemporary world no longer would tolerate his profession. The burdens of modern society had become too complex, the problems too critical, and the necessity for solutions too insistent to permit the

[5] Hans W. Weigert, "Oswald Spengler, Twenty-five Years After," *Foreign Affairs*, Vol. XXI (October, 1942), 120–21; Oron J. Hale, "The Dignity of History in Times of War," *Journal of Modern History*, Vol. XV (March, 1943), 1–6.

[6] Page Smith, *The Historian and History*, 56–57. For other comments about the popularity of attempts at universal history see John Higham in Higham *et al.*, *History*, 74; Ephraim A. Speiser, "The Ancient Near East and Modern Philosophies of History," American Philosophical Society *Proceedings*, Vol. 95 (1951), 583–88; John Wendon, "Christianity, History, and Mr. Toynbee," *Journal of Religion*, Vol. XXXVI (July, 1956), 139–49.

luxury of either antiquarian dabbling or the satisfaction of purely personal esthetic whims. Historians had to be more than ever concerned with the whys of history or abdicate in favor of amateur theorists or philosophers. In the early part of the century Henry Adams had warned that history must become scientific or face extinction. By 1942 that gloomy prediction seemed more and more relevant. Yet there were great dangers that any frantic re-examination might well destroy the historian's claim to objectivity so carefully nurtured for nearly one hundred years or that the temptation to utilize the crutches of other disciplines would prove irresistible.

With the memory of the World War I experience still fresh when historians enlisted in the causes of their respective nations as paid propagandists, Roy F. Nichols warned his colleagues that in wartime there is always heavy pressure to distort history in what is the seeming national interest. Peoples in crisis demand historical justifications for the sacrifices they are forced to make and the sufferings they are made to endure. The historian as citizen can well understand this need, for he shares it, but the great test of his historianship is to be found in his resistance to any perversion of the historical record. Nichols did conclude, however, that the historian must theorize about causes; he must interpret and explain.[7] Objectivity does not mean passivity and an indifference to the intellectual agony of the times.

For the historian in the middle twentieth century much of that pain resulted from the onrush of totalitarian systems which defied the premises of enlightened Western culture. Historians could not be expected to approve a mechanism which held in contempt the notion of free inquiry and which if allowed to triumph would signal the termination of his profession. In taking note of the threat, Frederick J. Teggart found that the answer for the historian lay in his own unique capacity to comprehend the reasons for events and personalities. The writer of history did not have to become either a polemical antagonist or a superpatriotic apologist in order to defend those ideals so essential to his calling and his society; he

[7] Roy F. Nichols, "Confusions in Historical Thinking," *Journal of Social Philosophy and Jurisprudence*, Vol. VII (July, 1942), 337.

could best serve that cause by simply practicing his vocation, that of being a historian. But being a historian, Teggart insisted, was primarily the searching for causes and explaining them to the public audience. It was a lonely quest. The historian could not and should not look to philosophy or mathematics or biology or physics.[8] By himself the historian must confront the past, for only he has the training and equipment to extract answers, or, more correctly, only the historian knows the proper questions to ask of the past. From this silent dialogue between the historian and his sources there might emerge fresh insights which could contribute to man's ability to survive, to find meaning in his own history, to gain at least a tentative wisdom, and to realize more poignantly than before the quality of being human.

At its most elemental level the world crisis has posed the question of literal human survival on the planet. The possibility of the extinction of human existence, always remotely theoretical in the past, has for modern man become a fact of life. It is one with which he must live on a daily basis. While his foreknowledge of personal death has always been realized by the individual, he has never had to face the question of the eradication of not only civilization but also the species itself. Adding to the trauma is the immediacy of the threat. Buttons may be pushed tomorrow or the next day or the day after that. In the light of such potential catastrophe the historian has asked himself if there is anything he can contribute to ensure the continuity of the race. Can comfort and solace be discovered in the study of history? Does history say anything to man caught in almost unbearable tension? Certainly the historian cannot remain unmoved or complacent. To follow the old familiar paths, to ask no new questions of the past, is to invite social and intellectual exile.[9] If man and his world are menaced by the movement of history, then those whose

[8] Frederick J. Teggart, "Causation in Historical Events," *Journal of the History of Ideas*, Vol. III (January, 1942), 3.

[9] C. Vann Woodward has observed that "if historians assume an intransigent attitude toward reinterpretation, they will deserve to be regarded as antiquarians and their history as irrelevant." C. Vann Woodward, "The Age of Reinterpretation," *American Historical Review*, Vol. LXVI (October, 1960), 18.

preoccupation is the study of history should be able to advance some effective explanations.

It is the historical nature of the crisis which permits some hope that historians can offer guidance and suggest remedies. According to one English historian, Western man has been "driven to ask fundamental questions about himself and his evolution to this perilous state. By and large, these are historical questions, for they involve the whole life of mankind on earth."[10] Nuclear fission was the result of historical process, as well as the product of the physicist's laboratory. Nazism did not like Venus from the brow of Jove leap full-grown from the mind of Hitler. Historical causation is not so simple; its strands extend back into remoter recesses of time, and an understanding of these processes can best be supplied by the historian, working at his craft. But he must constantly re-examine in knowledge of the present and in hope for the future.

It may seem paradoxical to insist that the concern of the historian must be for the future as well as the past, but on close examination there is really very little else which justifies the practice of historianship. This observation will undoubtedly offend those who find in the study and writing of history an aesthetic pleasure or those who advocate the history-for-history's-sake approach; yet it seems apparent that society tolerates the latter luxuries only if it can be promised more practical dividends. Yet it is not only the demands of society which dictate attention to the future but also that which is implicit in the study of history, itself. For what better guide to the actions of mankind, both individually and collectively, can be discovered than in the historical record? From the time of Thucydides onward historians have maintained that an examination of what has gone before can serve as an illuminant of the future. Since 1945 this assertion has taken on a deeper significance, a feeling by many that the study of history is the basic essential in the struggle for survival.

10 John C. Cairns, "The Historian in the Western World," *South Atlantic Quarterly*, Vol. LI (October, 1952), 504. This is not to maintain that only historians are capable of providing answers for contemporary society. Obviously, the skills of many others are required as well. What is being emphasized is the recognition of the special qualifications of historians to deal with problems that are, in part, historical.

For Page Smith it is "a means of making possible a decent future for all mankind."[11]

One reason for this faith is the obvious parallel which exists between the special condition of the historian and the general human condition. What has become increasingly clear to modern man has been his isolation. Having lost confidence in many of the securities of earlier ages, having discovered the vastness of the physical universe and his own consequent minuteness, and having been told of the uncharted depths of his own subconscious, modern man has come to realize the singularity of his experience. All that he has as an individual is himself and what he has experienced; all that he possesses as a society is history. Though true, it is irrelevant to complain that the history man knows is fragmentary, filled with prejudice, and, at best, uncertain as a guide for either present action or future prediction. It is all we have, and it must be used. And who is to say that, despite the admitted inadequacies of historical method and findings, researchers might not uncover fresh data and reinterpretations leading to a wisdom so necessary at the present time? Even a re-examination of what is already known might prove fruitful. "Some of us historians believe that, if more people knew more history and would heed it, past human experience could help create that better world so many have long wished for."[12]

There is, however, a great danger in using history as a guidepost for the present and future—believing that history repeats itself. This widely repeated aphorism has just enough truth to make it an easily believed cliché. Historical situations do recur; analogies with past events and personalities are commonplace. But history itself remains a chain which is endlessly varied and different. How could it be otherwise? Considering the multiple causative factors found in any historical situation, not to mention the roles played by individual and tremendously diverse personalities, it would seem impossible for exact historical repetition. What does happen is the recurrence of similar historical contexts, the reappearance of like personalities,

11 Smith, *The Historian and History*, 226.

12 Howard K. Beale, "The Professional Historian: His Theory and His Practice," *Pacific Historical Review*, Vol. XXII (August, 1953), 227.

and the continual interplay of familiar forces. When the historian adds to these variables certain constants, such as basic drives within human nature, he may be able to arrive at hypotheses which, while not accurate prophecies, can nevertheless be of substantive value in understanding current problems and providing the basis for intelligent planning for the future. But the lessons of history must be carefully handled, for the pitfalls of slavish attachment to them are obvious.

A good example is the mystique that has arisen from the appeasement of Hitler at Munich in 1938 over the Czechoslovakian crisis. Since the attempts by England's Neville Chamberlain to assuage the Nazi dictator's appetite proved futile and World War II ensued within the year, the lesson has been drawn that all appeasement efforts are valueless and lead only to war. Indeed, both the words "Munich" and "appeasement" have become synonymous for craven submission and cowardly retreat. The British prime minister's umbrella, the treaty paper which he waved so jubilantly to the throng at London Airport, the promise of "peace in our time" have become symbols of ignominious betrayal. To gain support for a particular policy or program, statesmen, diplomats, and politicians have continued to make heavy reference to the dangers of appeasement. The phrase "another Munich" has been consistently employed by both the Soviet Union and the United States in castigating the actions of each other and even of allies. Obviously one of the "lessons" of history drawn from the crisis of 1938 has been that appeasement is bad. But does a close examination of the historical record give credence to this assumption? The answer is not a simple yes or no. Everything depends upon the particular context and upon a definition of terms. If by appeasement one means accommodation, then history is replete with instances where such a course of action proved beneficial to all parties involved. Certainly, compromise, a retreat from hard demands or positions, is not always ignoble. There must also be considered the matter of personality and ideology. The appeasing of Hitler and the Nazi drive for dominion cannot be successfully compared to attempts to rectify justifiable grievances or to placate a ruler whose desires, while upsetting, may still be rooted in

23

basic political realities. Does this mean, then, that one can gain no instruction from a reading of history? No, but it does mean that the searcher after historical lessons cannot confine his examination of the past to a single event; he must peruse a broad spectrum of the record. It also implies that he would be well advised to rely on professional counsel. The truly qualified interpreter of history is the historian.

Perhaps the most important knowledge which the historian learns from history is the tentativeness and incompleteness of his knowledge; such recognition marks the beginning of wisdom. Yet he is sustained by the belief that his quest is not hopeless. The amassing of historical information is a cumulative process, and, while the historian often is engaged in a groping in semidarkness, there is always the possibility that his investigations may lead to additional light. Building upon all the work that has preceded his own, he can substantially, if slowly, widen the vistas of understanding for himself, his fellow craftsmen, and civilized society. The realization that his labors may be crucial to survival has become apparent to some who have demanded that historians face responsibility and provide guidance in this time of world crisis.

In 1947 the noted historian C. H. McIlwain said that the historian's obligation, though always a large one, had never been "so heavy as in this present era of change and uncertainty." Comparing the historian's activity to "some sort of a religious act," McIlwain asserted that if nations are to survive they "must guide their actions in light of earlier experience and of that experience the historian is our only interpreter." Boyd Shafer has added the admonition that historians must "fully live up to their potentialities and face their responsibilities" if they are to have any role in "determining whether this their world will continue, and, if so, in what human condition." But Shafer also has held out the golden promise that "historians of the twentieth century might come as close to the heavenly city as any scholars may."[13]

13 C. H. McIlwain, "The Historian," in R. B. Heywood (ed.), *The Works of The Mind*, 214; Boyd C. Shafer, "The Study of History in the United States," *AAUP Bulletin*, Vol. L (September, 1964), 240.

Both McIlwain and Shafer are in effect maintaining the need for presentism in historical study. The historian cannot isolate himself from contemporary life without abdicating the responsibility which has been assigned to him. He has a dual commitment: his professional duty and that of a concerned human being living in a world perilously close to self-annihilation. In each case he must recognize the inescapable fact which his own study teaches him, that "those who live merely in the past cannot survive in the present. The essence of that lesson is that history is not only then: it is now."[14]

Survival, of course, is much more than a simple continuing of physical existence. No matter how well historians do their job, no matter how well the lessons of history are absorbed and put to use, man can never return to a prenuclear age. He will continue to live on the edge of the abyss—one which contains not only the potentiality for the swift savagery of atomic devastation but also the possibility of the more insidious but no less deadly bacteriological contamination of the world. Can he surmount the tension inherent in that situation enough to allow himself sufficient tranquility for the good life? History, said Crane Brinton, "can offer a kind of consolation, that the bad as well as the good of everyday life is never wholly new and therefore, perhaps, never wholly unbearable. Not even the horrendous prospects of an end of the world . . . are wholly unique."[15] History, therefore, can demonstrate the community of man through the ages and the commonality of the human condition whether it was experienced in the ancient cities of Sumeria, the France of Louis XIV, or the metropolitan complexes of modern America. Problems viewed in perspective lose some of their terror, shed some of their pressing immediacy, and allow reason rather than panic to prevail. But history must demonstrate more than perspective; it must impart meaning to life as well.

The possibility of discerning meaning in history was by no means a new hope as philosophers, theologians, and historians in centuries

---

[14] A. S. Eisenstadt, "History Is Now," *Journal of Higher Education*, Vol. XXIX (October, 1958), 408.

[15] Crane Brinton, "Many Mansions," *American Historical Review*, Vol. LXIX (January, 1964), 324.

previous attempted to justify a creed, dogma, or theory on the basis of the historical evidence. Some, like Saint Augustine and Bishop Bossuet, saw in history the providential hand of God and the secular fulfillment of the Christian promise, while others, such as Karl Marx, perceived no intimation of divine intervention but did see an inevitability in the historical process leading to an ultimate utopia. Writers as disparate in time and personality as Giambattista Vico and Brooks Adams were able to detect patterns and cycles which operated in history. The record of mankind, whether viewed in sacred or profane context, has continually been used in an attempt to answer the ancient imponderables: Where have we been? Why are we here? Where are we going? The crises of the atomic age, however, led historians to a renewed introspection as they came to "realize that the question can be raised whether concern with history has any meaning in a world that is fundamentally changed from the world of the past."[16]

Postwar historians were aware of the clamor from both the public and their academic colleagues for a history which would offer some guidance and enlightenment in the new world of imminent catastrophe, though at first glance the problem appeared nearly insoluble. Nor did the immediate past record of the profession suggest optimism. Noting the poverty of the historical contribution toward "solving twentieth-century man's dilemma," John Bowditch typified the reaction of many writers when he suggested that the historian was hard-pressed to comprehend what had happened much less "deal with the tortured world in which he finds himself." Under such conditions there was an inclination on the part of some to adopt a protective fatalism, a kind of sophisticated despair based on the inevitability of the historical process. Such a frame of reference would absolve the historian of any responsibility. In a study of textbooks of European history Lacey Baldwin Smith discovered this attitude to be generally present. Smith deplored the tendency while understanding it and urged his compatriots to discard the pretense of fatalism, arguing that such attitudes were contradictory to the heart of historical study, being at their roots unhistorical.[17] Gener-

16 Felix Gilbert in Higham *et al.*, *History*, 384.
17 John Bowditch, "War and the Historian," in H. Stuart Hughes (ed.), *Teachers*

ally, historians responded to the demand for meaning in their studies and began to re-examine historical material in light of contemporary needs.

Most agreed that the essential ingredient was faith. Some preferred to find in history additional reasons for returning to the Christian interpretation of history, while others rejected the notion of a divine force manifesting itself through the centuries and placed their faith in strictly human endeavor. But all who sought meaning in history realized the necessity of first believing that meaning was possible. Those who found solace in the renaissance of Christian historiography could point with pride to the writings of the American Reinhold Niebuhr and three English writers, Christopher Dawson, Arnold Toynbee, and Herbert Butterfield. Perhaps the foremost spokesman for this school of thought in the United States was E. Harris Harbison, who spoke eloquently of the tragedy of our times and the necessity of finding meaning in that tragedy.[18] Especially has the popular acclaim given Toynbee's *A Study of History* been interpreted as "part of that general swing toward some kind, indeed several kinds of renewed faith in religion."[19]

Even those who made no effort to tie together religion and history taught the importance of belief and outlined ways in which historians could illuminate the past for the benefit of the present. Their position was best summarized recently by T. H. Von Laue, who urged his fellow craftsmen to write history "not for the profession but for a public of educated, thoughtful, and intelligent citizens who turn to history for light amidst the baffling or frightening darkness in their lives and times." The idea, expressed by Von Laue, that history can serve as a means of spiritual sustenance was earlier stated by Colin

---

of History, 320; Lacey Baldwin Smith, "A Study of Textbooks on European History During the Last Fifty Years," *Journal of Modern History*, Vol. XXIII (September, 1951), 250–56.

[18] Butterfield has given the best statement of the modern Christian historian's position in *Christianity and History*. For an elaboration of Harbison's viewpoint see his *Christianity and History: Essays* and "The Meaning of History and the Writing of History," *Church History*, Vol. XXI (1952), 97–107.

[19] Crane Brinton, "Toynbee's City of God," *Virginia Quarterly Review*, Vol. XXXII (Summer, 1956), 373.

Goodykoontz, who maintained that "history has the power along with religion, philosophy, literature, and the arts, to lift the spirit of man as it were to a mountain top from which he can more clearly take his bearings in a time of change and confusion."[20] There were already devices at hand to accomplish the mission, although there were differences of opinion about which was the most useful.

The principal debate concerning historical technique centered on the old argument between the narrative and the analytical approaches to the writing of history. The latter method, largely a bequest of the age of scientific historiography, attempted to utilize the scientific method with its emphasis upon observation and the accumulation of statistics. Roy F. Nichols, in comparing the period of the American Civil War and the present time as eras of maximum confusion, believed that the present capacity for understanding was considerably superior because the modern historian has "a greater capacity for observation and analysis today." H. Stuart Hughes has advocated a closer connection between the historian and the social scientist, believing that the methodological tools and models of sister disciplines can increase the precision of historical analysis. Whereas both Nichols and Hughes would increase the analytical powers of the historian in an effort to alleviate the confusion rampant in the study of history, J. H. Hexter would employ the more traditional narrative approach. Only the narrative historian, argued Hexter, can make intelligible to his readers the decisions which men make. Analytical history will not do in a world of upheaval, according to Hexter. It is within the framework of an unfolding story that understanding occurs, and understanding is the necessary prerequisite to meaning.[21] Whatever method was used, historians hoped that a discovery of meaning in history would lead to a greater wisdom both for the individual and for society.

20 T. H. Von Laue, "Is There a Crisis in the Writing of History?" *Bucknell Review*, Vol. XIV (December, 1966), 1; Colin B. Goodykoontz, "The Founding Fathers and Clio," *Pacific Historical Review*, Vol. XXIII (February, 1954), 123.

21 Roy F. Nichols, "History in a Self-governing Culture," *American Historical Review*, Vol. LXXII (January, 1967), 420; Hughes, "The Historian and the Social Scientist," *American Historical Review*, Vol. LXVI (October, 1960), 22; J. H. Hexter, *Reappraisals in History*, 39–40.

Admittedly, a definition of wisdom is, like other abstractions, difficult to compose and to make relevant to the practical concerns of existence. Too often we call something or someone wise which corresponds to our own prejudices and predispositions. Yet, for the historian, wisdom is always a broadening of perspective, a confronting of reality on its own terms, and an ever-increasing awareness of humanity's potentiality—for good as well as for ill. The historian would concede that increased knowledge does not in itself constitute wisdom, but he would contend that without the benefit of knowledge wisdom is unobtainable. It is the application of knowledge—for history the collective experience of mankind—that produces sagacity and an ability to transcend the limitations of time and space and to apply the lessons of the past to the problems of the present. What history has to offer in the acquisition of wisdom is more the maintenance of a special attitude than the accumulation of large bodies of facts. That special attitude which historians usually refer to as historical-mindedness not only allows the individual to comprehend the past within its own context but also permits one to view the present with a heightened sensitivity conditioned by perspective.

A number of historians have identified this facet of historical learning as the most valuable for contemporary society and have endeavored to awaken their fellow historians to a sense of urgency on its behalf. Recognizing that the time is short and that the obstacles are many, they have prodded the profession to recapture some of its earlier zeal and sense of mission.[22] To reclaim its lost utility, however, history needs to achieve a unity which has been dissipated by intramural quarrels and worse still, an indifference to the torments of the times. Historians, said William L. Langer, abdicated the task of providing understanding of the present through a knowledge of the past and left it "to the newspaper and radio commentators." Boyd Shafer felt that too much time was spent by historians on

[22] Julian R. Boyd, "A Modest Proposal to Meet an Urgent Need," *American Historical Review,* Vol. LXX (January, 1965), 342. Not only written history but also history teaching needed reinvigoration. See M. G. Baxter *et al., The Teaching of American History in High Schools,* 120–21.

issues which divide, hindering "the fullest application of historical thought during an era not only of international crises but crises of the mind when the contribution of historical intelligence to human understanding could be of crucial significance." The stakes were too great to allow petty disagreements or traditional ideas and methods to thwart the contributions which many believed were within the province of historians to make. Whether others, especially in the physical and natural sciences, believed in the practicality of historical information was immaterial; historians had seen the uses of history put to evil employment. Scores of examples came to mind: the deification of personality, as in the case of Hitler, Napoleon, and Stalin to name but a few; the glorification of the state and nationhood above the requirements of human dignity, as witnessed in the injustices of Western imperialism of the nineteenth and early twentieth centuries; and the manipulation of the historic past to justify war and greed. History, commented Folke Dovring, "is a virulent factor in political and social conflicts and a basic substance in the structure of our personalities." If, through history, the world was to become only a little wiser, it would have to recapture its reputation for dedication to the highest human values and aspirations.[23] No better articulation of this goal and the part to be played by the historian in its attainment has been made than that by John J. Van Nostrand:

> If one must relate the past to the present, and I know of no other reason for collecting and reviving it, this is the time. In time of fear which blinds, seek the truth which clears the eye. In time of suspicion which makes little distinction between friend and foe train the judgment which marks the battle lines, locates the enemy and conserves strength until a telling blow can be struck. In time of prejudice, be tolerant.[24]

Only by entering actively into the area of public discussion could

[23] William L. Langer, "The Historian and the Present," *Vital Speeches*, March 1, 1953, p. 313; Boyd C. Shafer, "The Study of History in the United States," *AAUP Bulletin*, Vol. L (September, 1964), 233; Folke Dovring, *History as a Social Science: An Essay on the Nature and Purpose of Historical Studies, V.* (Hereafter cited as *History as a Social Science.*)

[24] John J. Van Nostrand, "The Historian as Teacher," *Pacific Historical Review*, Vol. XXI (February, 1952), 120.

the postwar historian push the world toward a soberer understanding of itself, and only by recognizing that the study of history was intimately associated with the tragedy and joy of man, that it was a liberal art,[25] could the historian "reach for some tiny fragment of the wisdom so sorely needed."[26]

In short, the historians of the postwar world were rediscovering the significance of their craft in a world increasingly guided and influenced by the formulas and precepts of science. Ironically, they were finding that more than ever the kind of wisdom in demand was that which could only come from those studies which dealt with man. They could take consolation in the knowledge that they were not alone; their allies in the liberal arts also had a long tradition of humanistic involvement. However, the pursuit of truth, meaning, and wisdom would also involve the special capabilities of the historian himself. The present crisis of man was also his own crisis, one "in the sense that a new humanity with a sharpened awareness and a deeper consciousness is being forged."[27]

[25] Jacques Barzun, "History as a Liberal Art," *Journal of the History of Ideas*, Vol. VI (January, 1945), 88.

[26] Gottschalk, "A Professor of History in a Quandary," *American Historical Review*, Vol. LIX (January, 1954), 285.

[27] Frank E. Manuel, *Shapes of Philosophical History*, 149–50.

At the heart of the postwar self-analysis undertaken by historians in America was the attempt to give fresh answers to an ancient question: What is the function and purpose of historical study? Teachers of history have always been both confronted and irritated by that familiar query from their students, usually asked somewhat inelegantly in the words, "What good is it?" The irritation comes not from the validity of the question but rather from the difficulty in answering it, for, however it is phrased, it is a legitimate and important inquiry. In no other area of historiographical investigation in recent years has there been so much activity, an indication of the import attributed to the discussion by historians. In an uncertain world writers of history have labored to discover the value of history to contemporary affairs and sought to reassert the traditional proposition that the study of history was one of the keys to understanding. Three years before the bombs fell on Pearl Harbor the eminent historian Guy S. Ford, anticipating the postwar trend, stated that a successful confrontation by Americans with the forces of modern society would come "only because history reclaims its proper place as the most trustworthy guide to the study and interpretation of human conduct."[1]

Traditionally, the historian has been one of the agents to which mankind has entrusted its past, the chief function of his art being that of acting as society's collective memory and as the guardian and conservator of its values. It is a task which he has shared with the poet, the storyteller, and the mythmaker. Indeed, the great historian has often embodied in his own craft many of the attributes

1 Guy S. Ford, "Some Suggestions to American Historians," *American Historical Review*, Vol. XLIII (January, 1938), 267.

which characterize his colleagues in the recalling of ancient times and men. What has made him distinctive, of course, has been his devotion to accuracy and a desire to preserve the record of the past as nearly as possible to its actuality. Thucydides early recognized this special quality when he distinguished his own undertaking from that of the "lays of a poet displaying the exaggeration of his craft" and the "compositions of the chroniclers that are attractive at truth's expense." The great Athenian also saw clearly a problem which has plagued writers of history ever since, namely that of retaining interest in a narrative which aimed not at romance but at truth.

The historian also had to face the fact that in the exercise of his function he would at times come up against the unpleasant certainty of frequent human resistance to the truth about himself and his past. Often men would prefer to be reminded of their days of glory rather than of their hours of failure. That is one reason why the poet is more often celebrated than the historian and why the myth is simpler to enshrine than the historical record. It was likewise obvious that the historian would be more in demand at one time than at another. As has been earlier noted, times of crisis are much more likely to call forth the need for stability. When the future seems especially unknowable and the texture of existence the most tenuous, the historian is much more esteemed. When old ideals and principles seem endangered, the historian is in a strategic position, for he reminds his audience of its heritage and of the durability of the old values.[2] His message, unlike that of the scientist or the philosopher, has usually been transmitted in narrative form, resulting in a closer rapport between the writer of history and his readers. The loss of communication since the rise of scientific historiography may well be traceable to the decreasing emphasis upon narrative in preference for the analytical. Some historians writing since 1945 have suggested that the retention of the narrative form may be in itself an important function of history.

The most obvious and natural justification for the telling of history as a story is that this is the way it presents itself to the onlooker.

[2] Max Farrand, "The Quality of Distinction," *American Historical Review*, Vol. XLVI (April, 1941), 521.

Using his own personal experience as a reference point, the student of history cannot help but see the past as unfolding from a particular point in time to another, posterior point. This viewpoint was reinforced in the western world by the Judaeo-Christian concept of the linear movement of history. For the Israelite, God's promises were to be fulfilled in time, the acquisition of the Promised Land and the coming of the Kingdom were to be historical events; for the Christian, the birth, life, and death of Christ were not mythical re-enactments of some ancient legends but unique actualities which had occurred at a certain time and place. Moreover, the redemption which he had pledged to his followers was to come at the end of history, which was a point in the future. What was more natural than to relate in narrative fashion something which had beginnings and ends and which seemed to move from cause to effect, from birth to death. It was not just that narrative appeared to be history's normal habiliment, however, but additionally that the telling of a story attracted a wider audience. And if history was to be useful, it first had to be read.

As early as 1943 that gadfly of historians Bernard De Voto had warned writers of history that by divorcing history from its story they were causing a loss of interest in what was "the most interesting of all subjects." Later J. H. Hexter wrote that "many of us have got so preoccupied with analysis and argumentation that we are in danger of forgetting how to tell a story and even of forgetting that telling a story is the historian's real business after all." The idea that narration was the historian's "real business" struck a forgotten but responsive chord within the profession, for historians knew that this was the way their craft had originated, with the storyteller. "Historians may aspire to science," stated A. S. Eisenstadt, "but their highest calling is that of troubadours and of bards, of minne-singers and of Homers."[3]

The critical point observed by both professional and popularizer alike was the intimacy which existed between the narrative form

---

[3] Bernard De Voto, "The Easy Chair," *Harper's*, Vol. CLXXXVII (July, 1943), 132; Hexter, *Reappraisals in History*, 21; Eisenstadt, "American History and Social Science," in Eisenstadt (ed.), *The Craft of American History*, II, 117.

and the essential vitality of written history. Without the tension which is produced when events are presented in a sequential fashion, without the presence of suspense and the unexpected which are the ingredients of any successful story, history became lifeless. Barbara Tuchman maintained that "narrative is the life-blood of history; it is the vehicle that carries it, the medium through which the historian communicates what he has to tell." C. Vann Woodward has compared the work of the historian to the playwright and the novelist and has urged his fellow historians to remember that his problems are those he has "in common with all storytellers," the most significant of which is "keeping his audience interested." Even the intellectual historian, said John C. Greene, should not be exempt from writing a narrative which "not only tells what happened and why it happened but makes it happen again for the reader."[4]

Though aware of the insistence for more dramatic narrative, historians were unwilling for the most part to disengage themselves entirely from the goals and attitudes inherited and so deeply absorbed from scientific historiography. The concept that the truly legitimate function of history was to recreate the past as it really had been remained a strong and significant element in historical thought. Gone, perhaps, was the supreme confidence that the totality of history could be in fact recaptured, but there still remained the belief that through the rigorous application of historical methodology enough of the remains of the past could be reclaimed to offer a decently objective and comprehensive historical picture. Placing much trust in the validity of historical "facts," many historians continued to preach that the final goal of the writer of history was to get at the truth of things through a systematic accretion of knowledge.

"The historian's basic task," asserted Samuel Eliot Morison, "is one of presenting a corpus of ascertained fact," and all philosophical speculation concerning the limitations of scientific history should not

4 Barbara Tuchman, "Can History Be Served Up Hot?" *New York Times Book Review*, March 8, 1964, p. 30; C. Vann Woodward, *The Burden of Southern History*, 27; C. Vann Woodward, "The Age of Reinterpretation," *American Historical Review*, Vol. LXVI (October, 1960), 18–19; Greene, "Objectives and Methods in Intellectual History," *Mississippi Valley Historical Review*, Vol. XLIV (June, 1967), 67.

"obscure this plain, outstanding principle." The main function of the historian, observed John J. Van Nostrand, "is to get at the truth. Here he owes his supreme obligation." Both Richard Bauer and Max Savelle emphasized the empirical nature of historical study and, while admitting that the labors of the historian took him into more speculative areas, argued in favor of the objectivity of historical knowledge.[5] The faith that such knowledge could be obtained was based heavily upon the acceptance of the historical method as a scientific tool which was as valid for ancient as for modern history.[6] The efficacy of the method assured the reliability of the data. If enough work was done in the investigation of any particular era or period, the approach to a "total" picture of the age under consideration would be made. Such objective researchers would concede that not every last scrap of the past was recoverable, but they would insist that "the historian can produce estimates of 'total situations.' "[7]

Other historians, although in agreement with their more confident colleagues about the reliability of historical data, were less sure about the nature of the result. Crane Brinton preferred to compare the work of the historian to that of the cartographer. "The map is not the piece of earth itself, not 'reality.' It has, however, a readily verifiable relation with the piece of earth it maps." Brinton's analogy, which defined written history as a representation of reality rather than reality itself, nevertheless indicated that it was possible to see a given time in history within a total context. This idea received an illuminating presentation in an article by John T. Marcus, who found in the very nature of the historical discipline an ability to get

[5] Samuel Eliot Morison, "The Faith of a Historian," *American Historical Review*, Vol. LVI (January, 1951), 263; Van Nostrand, "The Historian as Teacher," *Pacific Historical Review*, Vol. XXI (February, 1952), 113; Richard H. Bauer, "The Study of History," *Social Studies*, Vol. XXXIX (April, 1948), 156; Max Savelle, "The Philosophy of the General: Toynbee Versus the Naturalists," *Pacific Historical Review*, Vol. XXV (February, 1956), 63.

[6] Nichols, "Postwar Reorientation of Historical Thinking," *American Historical Review*, Vol. LIV (October, 1948), 87.

[7] Richard Challener and Maurice Lee, Jr., "History and the Social Sciences: The Problem of Communications," *American Historical Review*, Vol. LXI (January, 1956), 335–36. Quincy Wright has stated that "history seeks to recreate the total life of the nation or civilization." Review of Sir Charles Petrie, *Diplomatic History, 1713–1933*, in *American Historical Review*, Vol. LVI (October, 1950), 71.

glimpses of "transcending wholeness" because of the combination of causal and configurational analysis. More mundane was the hope held out by J. H. Hexter, who maintained that through a process of constant re-examination the historian can achieve "piecemeal advances" and a clearer vision of an epoch as his "vocabulary of conceptions" improves.[8] However much historians still sought to validate the reality of their facts and the objectivity of their knowledge, the primary thrust of historical thought since World War II has been toward a presentist orientation which would emphasize both the immediacy and the utility of history.

One of the more familiar justifying arguments used to support historical study has been the contention that the study of history has practical application for both the present and the future. The idea that lessons are to be learned and instruction to be gained from knowledge of the past has long been the staple argument for the inclusion of history within the school curriculum, and the popularity of history with the general public has been largely dependent upon the maintenance of this belief.[9] In fact, so repetitious has been its expression that any assertion of the contemporaneity of history appears hackneyed and a restatement of the obvious. Furthermore, those historians, fully committed to the certitudes of scientific history, were often unsympathetic to any suggestion that seemed to imply a teleology or to anything which might deprive the discipline of total objectivity. In the rethinking of the profession and its problems which has taken place since 1945, historians have felt it necessary to dress the old idea in new clothes and to redefine its relevance to present society. The critical point in the new analysis was the acceptance of the notion that "historical study is a form of self-consciousness."[10] If this is true, the writing and reading of

[8] Crane Brinton, "Something Went Wrong: Three Views of the Heritage of the Early 19th Century," *Journal of the History of Ideas*, Vol. XIV (June, 1953), 462; John T. Marcus, "The Changing Consciousness of History," *South Atlantic Quarterly*, Vol. LX (Spring, 1961), 225; Hexter, *Reappraisals in History*, 202.

[9] J. Franklin Jameson, "The Future Uses of History," *American Historical Review*, Vol. LXV (October, 1959), 62–63.

[10] A. S. Eisenstadt, "Introductory Notes," in Eisenstadt (ed.), *The Craft of American History*, II, 3.

history is a calculated activity of the present, one of its objects being the acquisition of insight and information leading to a deeper understanding of the past in the present. Page Smith stated the case for the advocates of a presentist orientation when he argued that "only by being relevant to his day and age has [the historian] the remotest chance of being relevant to any future day."[11]

The admonition of Socrates that the unexamined life is not worth living has had special applicability to postwar historians who have contended that a crucial part of the examination should include history. By adding depth and dimension to existence and by making the individual aware of the immense totality of the human experience which has preceded him, history can serve as an effective counterweight to the ennui which has so characterized modern life. Like T. S. Eliot and Dante, who saw in boredom a rejection of life itself, historians have often perceived the study of history as ultimate humanism, as an embracing of the principle of life, and consequently, as decisive affirmation in a world not infrequently dominated by negativism. The understanding of the present can only be nourished by a knowledge of the past, and "remembered experience, knowledge of history, is the beginning of understanding, of intelligent action and enjoyable thought." History is a comforter despite its tragedy and farce, for, as Felix Gilbert said, it "reasserts the role of man in a world that appears to slide out of human control." It may well be no guide to present action, nor would many maintain that problems are solved by historical guidelines or analogies, but the historian can explain similar problems of the past without the myopia induced by contemporary irritations. Life, indeed, can be more meaningful when the observation of Jacques Maritain is accepted that, although the present has its own reality, historical principles remain constant.

For the individual who is concerned about present and future, who attempts to examine, in the Socratic sense, the enigma of man, history, believed Richard Sullivan, can lead him to the fundamental questions: "the possibility of rational action, the location of the boundary separating necessity from freedom in human affairs, the role of the creative effort in the social order, and possibilities of

11 Smith, *The Historian and History*, 228.

escape from a routinized existence dictated by a mechanized society."[12] History is not a substitute for abstract principle;[13] it is not a religion; but it is a beginning toward a richer life.

Another presentist argument is that a knowledge of history is an indispensable ingredient for society when it attempts to define and analyze its social aims. The only trustworthy guide, it is claimed, in deciding the proper programs for the present is the record of the past. Indeed, many would maintain that history is the only guide, for it is the solitary purveyor of the empirical experience necessary to direct conduct. In such a context the relevance of all history becomes apparent; nothing is remote, for the problems of the Athenians in the fifth century before Christ or those of the Romans in the waning days of the Republic may provide more useful analogues than those extracted from more recent times. A careful scrutiny of the past, conducted by the professional historian, is also of obviously greater merit and utility than a historical ransacking undertaken by the untutored. The real question is not *whether* the past will be used but rather *who* will do it, "for the world depends on history for the basis of all its social policies and laws."[14] The historian then, said Conyers Read, cannot escape his social responsibility; he must justify himself and his craft in social terms.[15] How enlightened is his own society depends in large measure on the availability, attractiveness, and accuracy of the history the historian records.

The plea for the social utility of historical information was also a facet of a larger belief in its rationalizing quality, in its ability to

[12] Boyd C. Shafer, "The Historian in America," *Southwestern Historical Quarterly*, Vol. LX (January, 1957), 385–86; Felix Gilbert in Higham *et al.*, *History*, 387; H. C. Nixon, "Paths to the Past: The Presidential Addresses of the Southern Historical Association," *Journal of Southern History*, Vol. XVI (February, 1950), 38; William J. Grace, "Jacques Maritain and Modern Catholic Historical Scholarship," *Journal of the History of Ideas*, Vol. V (October, 1944), 445; Richard E. Sullivan, "Clio in the Classroom," *Centennial Review*, Vol. VII (Summer, 1963), 373.

[13] C. Vann Woodward, quoted in *Time*, March 29, 1954, pp. 40–41.

[14] Clarence P. Gould, "History—A Science?" *Mississippi Valley Historical Review*, Vol. XXXII (December, 1945), 378.

[15] Conyers Read, "The Social Responsibilities of the Historian," *American Historical Review*, Vol. LV (January, 1950), 279. See also Eisenstadt, "American History and Social Science," in Eisenstadt (ed.), *The Craft of American History*, II, 111, 117.

foster a certain cast of mind which was logical and reflective. In an age in which the irrational and the violent were pervasive, at a time when the demands for coolness and quietude of thought were never more compelling, the study of history was considered by some to be the necessary sedative to produce sufficient tranquillity in order that rationality might assert itself. "No society," declared Arthur Bestor, "can move forward in a rational way until the members composing it have attempted to comprehend the historical forces that brought their society into being."[16] Without an understanding of these factors men often tend to ignore the pluralistic origins of contemporary life and to be seduced by monistic theories which reduce the processes of history to a dialectic that ignores the fertility and variety of the past. A major characteristic of the cultivated mind is its capacity to admit the new and the unknown in a manner that is still consonant with a sense of fundamental value.[17] History allows this process to occur; it permits a historical sensibility to develop which must be present if rationality is to exist.

A corollary to the idea that a knowledge of history is a prerequisite for civilized rationality is the belief that such knowledge may also be expertly utilized in the decision making of statesmen and political leaders. This is a familiar presentist argument, and one that has not been without its champions since World War II. Thomas A. Bailey has been the most outspoken advocate of this position. In his excellent analysis of Woodrow Wilson and the making of the peace at the conclusion of World War I, Bailey wrote with an eye toward the impending termination of World War II and the problems which the peacemakers would confront. "I am presenting this narrative," he said, "from the American point of view and with emphasis on what went wrong, in the hope that we may better recognize certain disastrous pitfalls, and not stumble into them again."[18] While admitting that history did not repeat itself,

16 Arthur Bestor, "The Humaneness of History," in Eisenstadt (ed.), *The Craft of American History*, I, 9.

17 Harvey Wish, "The American Historian and the New Conservatism," *South Atlantic Quarterly*, Vol. LXV (Spring, 1966), 191; Leonard Krieger in Higham *et al.*, *History*, 313.

18 Thomas A. Bailey, *Woodrow Wilson and the Great Betrayal*, v.

Bailey nevertheless declared that "I happen to be among those who believe that history has lessons for those who will read."[19] John D. Hicks voiced similar sentiments when he defined history as the "accumulated experience of mankind" which, if properly used, could contribute to "wise decisions" and "can save mankind from many potential disasters." The demurrer that since historical knowledge is only partial knowledge it is an unsure guide to present action was accepted by W. T. Laprade, who, while admitting the limitation, insisted that history "nevertheless pervades our time and cannot be escaped." The function of the historian, insisted Laprade, was to help his society understand its history better. The role of historian as counselor to a troubled age was further urged by Crane Brinton in his presidential address to the American Historical Association in 1964. He ridiculed the notion that history has no lessons to teach, observing that "if we cannot learn from history, many of us moderns, and certainly the Enlightened, aren't going to learn at all."[20]

To those who argued the relevance of history and its study to the present, one of the better, if less often cited, of their observations was the statement that historical knowledge was not a static accumulation which remained the same from one generation to the next. While the past as actuality is frozen in time, human knowledge and understanding of that past constantly increase, and thus, as our conception of the past is altered by new discoveries and interpretations, so the relationship of past to present is changed. An ever-broadening mass of information enhances the experience of the whole race and widens the available limits for intelligent decision. This relationship may be readily discerned in the natural and physical sciences, where the building of concepts visibly depends upon the labors of previous investigators, but it is not as clearly apparent for history. The findings of Lewis Namier, for example, concerning the structure of British politics in the eighteenth century not only have forced historians to revise many of their prior assumptions about

19 Thomas A. Bailey, *Woodrow Wilson and the Lost Peace, v.*

20 John D. Hicks, "What's Right with the History Profession," *Pacific Historical Review*, Vol. XXV (May, 1956), 111; W. T. Laprade, "Obstacles in Studying History," *South Atlantic Quarterly*, Vol. LIX (Spring, 1960), 214; Brinton, "Many Mansions," *American Historical Review*, Vol. LXX (January, 1965), 320.

Parliament and the party system in England but also have suggested a new historical methodology adaptable to the contemporary scene and offered a new vantage point for studying the politics of the modern era. Certainly the great Belgian historian Henri Pirenne contributed much to our picture of the medieval world with his insight into the significance of Islam's expansion on the Christian civilization of Western and Central Europe. Additionally, Pirenne made it impossible for future historians to ignore the dynamic economic forces which have so much to do with the shaping of society.

In American historiography the impact of Charles A. Beard's *Economic Interpretation of the Constitution* on the writing and study of history was truly monumental. Despite its admitted defects and the controversy it engendered, the Beardian thesis proved to be a creative implement for both the professional historian and the sophisticated public interested in reform and the freshness of a new approach to the Constitution and the application of constitutional law. The latter illustration demonstrates the commonplace fact that present interests often dictate the direction of historical research, but that does not negate the validity of the knowledge so acquired, nor does it necessarily cause doubt about the objectivity of the investigator. It does point up the very close connection between past and present and the creative activity of the historian who is a part of both.[21] The historian, said Hans Kohn, retrieves lost events and injects them into the "stream of human consciousness," where they become a part of present existence and exercise a broadening effect upon our understanding and actions. Chester M. Destler declared that "pure research, so-called, is as necessary in history to provide a body of constantly widening knowledge to those who

[21] One of the best statements regarding the creative function of the historian was made in an editorial entitled "History as a Living Art," in *Saturday Review of Literature*, September 4, 1948, p. 20. It said in part: "Perhaps it may be well to remember that history after all is a part of the present, the slipstream eddying behind the propellor of our collective lives as we make our way painfully into the future; that each age writes its history in its own image, because it has need of it; that this being so, it is the duty of an historian to cultivate objectivity without ever forgetting at any point that the history he is writing has a creative function for the years in which he is living."

would employ it in literature, the arts, industry and the world of affairs as it is for other academic disciplines."[22]

Not all historians, of course, subscribed to a presentist orientation in the writing of history. Many were unsympathetic to any historiographical concept which attempted to use history to answer current questions or explain contemporary problems. Raymond P. Stearns feared that such preoccupations would ruin genuine perspective and destroy historical-mindedness, while Dwight Hoover advised that questions other than those immediately relevant to the present also need to be asked. J. H. Hexter perhaps made the strongest statement along these lines when he maintained that a study of the past was valuable only in understanding more about the past and not in providing a model for present action or in outlining the future. Yet it would seem that most historians of the postwar period agreed with Martin Duberman that "if history cannot be perfectly relevant, it can be partially so," and with Leo Solt, who felt that the historian, like Janus, must reach a happy compromise of looking both to the past and to the present.[23]

Another function traditionally attributed to the study of history has been the acquisition of perspective by its students. The wise man, it has been assumed, owes much of his wisdom to an awareness of the grand scope of human experience, a sense of the continuity of human development that compels the thoughtful individual to see his own times within the larger framework of historical evolution. When confronted by the tragedies and glories of ages long dead, the possibilities of comparison and contrast are enhanced, the present becomes more endurable because of its similarities with the past, and

[22] Hans Kohn, "A Historian's Creed for Our Own Time," *South Atlantic Quarterly*, Vol. LII (July, 1953), 341; Chester M. Destler, "Some Observations on Contemporary Historical Theory," *American Historical Review*, Vol. LV (April, 1950), 524.

[23] Raymond P. Stearns, "College History and Its 'New Approaches,'" *School and Society*, Vol. LXXXII (August 20, 1955), 54–55; Dwight W. Hoover, "Some Comments on Recent United States Historiography," *American Quarterly*, Vol. XVII (Summer, 1965), 318; Hexter, *Reappraisals in History*, 187; Martin Duberman, "The Limitations of History," *Antioch Review*, Vol. XXV (Summer, 1965), 296; Leo F. Solt, "Some Reflections upon the Study of English History," *Social Studies*, Vol. XLVIII (March, 1957), 76.

the future less terrifying for, with history, one is not peering into an unknowable void but at least can perceive the outlines and shapes of things to come, however dim. Historical perspective, to be sure, is not the single ingredient of human wisdom, but it is one of the most necessary components and one of the most difficult to acquire.

The perspective gained by the study of history seems to be inextricably combined with the qualities of understanding and wisdom, attributes of which so much is spoken and so little known. Indeed, James L. Sellers has declared that historical study is "socially justifiable only on the basis of serving to broaden the understanding and sharpen the wisdom of society."[24] Such statements soon acquire the character of aphorisms and go largely unchallenged; but for the historian the truth or falsity of Sellers' assertion is of vital concern; his acceptance by the society in which he lives as well as his own self-image depends upon its reliability. Recently some historians have investigated the kind of understanding and wisdom which the study of history provides and have concluded that these virtues can only be captured through a knowledge of the polarities of human experience visibly and dramatically demonstrated in history.

The first of these extremes is the totality of the human record. To be able to categorize people and events into "eras" and "ages," to detect patterns and types, to note similar conditions of civilizations and nations are all examples of a higher human capacity to reflect upon its own condition and, furthermore, demonstrate the desire to impose some kind of order upon the past. History is not the only device for accomplishing this goal, but Edward Bennett maintained that "history, avoiding both excessive artistry and excessive abstraction represents the most careful attempt to give the whole unvarnished experience of the past."[25] For any comprehension to come from the study of history, it must be seen in its entirety. The grand sweep of man in time, the view of the panorama which witnessed the slow yet amazing spectacle of the trek from savagery to civilization,

[24] James L. Sellers, "Before We Were Members—The MVHA," *Mississippi Valley Historical Review*, Vol. XL (June, 1953), 21.

[25] Edward Bennett, "History and Science," *Social Science*, Vol. XXVII (June, 1952), 137. It is this quality, Bennett stated, that gives us perspective.

and the even slower journey to some spiritual and psychological insight are absolutely necessary to the requirements of perspective. History exists in the macrocosm, and those who refuse to perceive it in its broadest angle of vision blind themselves to a significant part of its capacity to enlighten and instruct. One need not be a historicist to accept the principle that any point in history has reference points which came before, in some cases long before. The rise of Hitler and Nazism was not just a phenomenon explainable only in terms of the depression of the thirties or even in the political instability of the Weimar Republic; its roots go much deeper, some of which extend to those primeval German forests familiar to the "germ" theorists of the last century. Human institutions as well as individuals are the sums of their histories, and the historian must see them whole.

Counterbalancing the need to conceive the past in broad terms, the study of history also permits the student to acquire another element basic to perspective: the ability to grasp the particularity of things. It is commonplace but nevertheless true that everything in history is unique, that history does not repeat itself, and that a historical event or personage in order to be understood must be accepted pretty much on its own terms. This quality of historical-mindedness is based upon the particular nature of historical episodes, upon the variety of circumstance and personality which gives to each event its own unique set of accidents that sets it apart from other and similar occurrences. It is profitable to be able to compare the election of 1896 with that of 1932, to see likenesses in candidates and platforms; but historical veracity will be the loser if each campaign is not also explained within the context of its own times, with conditions peculiar to that specific time and place. William McKinley and Herbert Hoover shared similar beliefs, 1896 and 1932 were both depression years, and William Jennings Bryan and Franklin D. Roosevelt appealed strongly to the rural South; but 1896 was not 1932, and the historian who allows glib generalities and the superficialities of comparable situations to dominate his attention commits as serious an offense as does he who refuses to make comparisons or analogies. History in microcosm gives its readers "a consciousness of particular circumstances in human affairs and teaches them to be wary of broad generalizations and quick solutions."[26] From the knowledge that the historical record is so complex and various comes an intellectual modesty necessary to understanding with perspective.[27]

Historians have also held that those habits of mind commensurate with balance and judiciousness may be inculcated through the practice of the historical method. Clifford Lord, in pointing to the values of studying local history, said that history can teach us to weigh conflicting evidence to perceive the deliberate lie, to recognize propaganda and the misrecollection, and finally to grant perspective by being able to gauge "how far we have come and how fast." Boyd Shafer has suggested presciently that the greatest function of history has been to give man a sense of alternatives in any given situation, thus enhancing an individual's (or an institution's) freedom by increasing his options. Too frequently the historian is concerned only with what *did* happen; he must likewise be aware of what *did not* occur. This awareness will of necessity alert him to the complexities of decision making and the prevalence of choice. History reveals the burden of responsibility carried by men and the fragility of their lives. Perspective can be the result.[28]

Finally, history can induce a sense of calm, without which perspective is impossible. In an age of anxiety history can be an antidote to fear and frustration by demonstrating the commonality of the human condition in other times and places. "It may well be that historical continuity gives human beings some assurance of immortality." Certainly "it fortifies our judgment in dealing with problems of the present and measuring our hopes for the future." With calmness comes clarity of vision, balance in judgment, and perspective in attitude. Roy F. Nichols asserted that the study of history

[26] William E. Simons, "The Study of History and the Military Leader," *Military Affairs*, Vol. XXVI (Spring, 1962), 25.

[27] This point is further developed by Golo Mann, "How Not to Learn from History," *Yale Review*, Vol. XLI (March, 1952), 389–90. "The study of history is the best antidote against all fanaticism, all extremism, all self-righteousness."

[28] Clifford L. Lord, "Localized History in the Age of Explosions," *North Carolina Historical Review*, Vol. XL (April, 1963), 228; Boyd C. Shafer, "History, Not Art, Not Science, but History," *Pacific Historical Review*, Vol. XXIX (May, 1960), 166.

holds especial pertinence for Americans in that the perspective so gained may finally release us from the "clutches of a heedless optimism," lead us to ethical and philosophical stabilization, "enable society to recall and reinforce concepts of moral values," and contribute to the preservation of man's liberty.[29] This claim may be expecting too much, but without history and the perspective it engenders, nothing can be expected.

Closely allied to the function of perspective, especially to the facility of being able to look at the total historical record, is the proposition that the historian should make meaningful generalizations about his reading and research.[30] This idea obviously did not originate with the historians of the postwar period; it is nearly as old as history itself. The Greek and Roman writers of history were quick to generalize, sometimes on the most meager evidence, and any school of historiography which was the least didactic in its aims generalized by necessity. In fact the only period in which this historical perogative was seriously questioned was when the advocates of "scientific" history dominated historical thought during the latter half of the nineteenth century, but it would be a mistake to assume that even then historians of the scientific persuasion made no generalizations at all. Yet there was the tendency, particularly in the United States, to think of the historian as primarily a fact gatherer rather than as a thinker or interpreter of the past to the present. What scientific historians in America seemed to object to most was the kind of sweeping generalization made by literary historians like Francis Parkman, who in his volumes describing the Anglo-French conflict in the New World explained the final French defeat as the cumulative result of a feminine national character, a royal absolutism

[29] Mark M. Krug, "History and the Social Sciences: The Narrowing Gap," *Social Education*, Vol. XXIX (December, 1965), 515; Samuel F. Bemis, "American Foreign Policy and the Blessings of Liberty," *American Historical Review*, Vol. LXVII (January, 1962), 291; Nichols, "Postwar Reorientation of Historical Thinking," *American Historical Review*, Vol. LIV (October, 1948), 87–89.

[30] In 1963 the Social Science Research Council devoted an entire volume to its study of the problem of generalization. See Louis Gottschalk (ed.), *Generalization in the Writing of History: A Report of the Committee on Historical Analysis of the Social Science Research Council.* (Hereafter cited as *Generalization in the Writing of History.*)

which refused to allow democracy to grow, and an enervating religious paternalism which similarly drained the national energy. However, with the rise of the self-styled "new history," clustered about the work of James Harvey Robinson, Carl Becker, and Harry Elmer Barnes, many of the tenets of the scientific school were challenged, including the question whether or not the historian ought to indulge in the practice of generalizing. The matter was further complicated by the relativist controversy of the twenties and thirties, but the outbreak of World War II and the age of crisis which it inaugurated convinced most historians that generalization in their work was necessary to the society in which they lived. There have been few points upon which there has been such general agreement among historians since 1945.

The basic contention has been that the making of generalizations is inherent within the very nature of the historian's craft, that it is a duty he can avoid only by ceasing to be a historian in the fullest sense of the word. The fundamental distinction between the chronicler and the writer of history lies precisely in the refusal of the former to ask any questions of his materials, to arrange them in anything more than a chronological sequence, or to convey any sense of direction to the motion of history. If the function of the historian is only to act as a mirror as M. I. Finley indicated, "the chronicle is the only correct form for his work. But if it is to understand . . . then it is to generalize, for every explanation is or implies one or more generalizations." The adoption of the slightest intent to extract the reasons for any historical episode leads inevitably to the making of generalizations, and there would be few historians who would permit themselves a historiographical concept of such restriction. Those who claim the absence of any metaphysic in their scholarship leave themselves "open to charges of deceit or triviality." The very nature of historical research is "a quest for meaning; and the historian is therefore, by necessity, a patternmaker."[31]

[31] M. I. Finley, "Generalizations in Ancient History," in Gottschalk (ed.), *Generalization in the Writing of History*, 34; Charles F. Mullett, "The Novelist Confronts Clio," *South Atlantic Quarterly*, Vol. LX (Winter, 1960), 68; W. B. Willcox, "An Historian Looks at Social Change," in Eisenstadt (ed.), *The Craft of American History*, I, 31–32.

The necessity of generalization has been further increased by the position in which the historian finds himself at the present time. Richard Schlatter has argued that the historian has been forced to take the place of the philosopher and the literary critic for contemporary society, for the aforementioned no longer ask the big questions, those matters which are the interests of all men. "The historian," maintained Charles N. Glaab, "is in a sense, a secular theologian, who justifies society, rather than the universe, to man."[32] Such a lofty position carries with it a goodly amount of social responsibility; secular theology is a serious undertaking and not one which can be dismissed either lightly or flippantly. Some historians, like Conyers Read, have accepted the burden gladly inasmuch as they have long advocated the social significance of the historian, while others, like Louis Gottschalk, have shouldered the responsibility more in response to what they see as an inescapable demand of society. There is no denying that the historian will meet his duties imperfectly; such is the nature of his work. His conclusions may often be misleading and in some cases wrong; but he should welcome, claimed Roy Nichols, the opportunity "to project himself beyond his tested data." For it was only by stretching himself that he could grow intellectually and become an increasingly important part of society.[33]

Avery Craven has made the best case for the application of meaningful generalization in historical writing. In a revealing article, written in 1952 for the *Journal of Southern History*, Craven contended that the "historian's job is to find order in a disorderly world." Perhaps the most controversial part of the statement was the author's argument that the threads to a pattern must be sought "whether they exist or not." Most historians would take issue with the idea that the

[32] Richard Schlatter, "Foreword," in Higham *et al.*, *History*, vii; Charles N. Glaab, "The Historian and the American Urban Tradition," in Eisenstadt (ed.), *The Craft of American History*, II, 35.

[33] Read, "The Social Responsibilities of the Historian," *American Historical Review*, Vol. LV (January, 1950), 276; Gottschalk, "A Professor of History in a Quandary," *American Historical Review*, Vol. LIX (January, 1954), 279; Nichols, "History in a Self-governing Culture," *American Historical Review*, Vol. LXXII (January, 1967), 423.

writer of history must function as a mythmaker for society, but Craven insisted that social sanity was dependent upon the perception of a rational universe and that it was the historian's duty to provide that assurance.[34] In a world seeming to slide ever further out of joint, the pressure for asserting intelligible human control over the myriad forces which beset mankind has come to be seen as a desirable imperative. A principal technique employed by the historian to provide understanding and meaning is making generalizations. Not all historians would subscribe to making their work a surrogate for philosophy, ethics, and religion; but few would deny that an important part of their function is the attempt to find some kind of meaning, however limited, through generalization.

Any generalization, of course, involves implicitly the making of a value judgment, which, as the relativists have been fond of pointing out, depends in no small part upon the historian's own frame of reference. This is particularly true when the historian attempts to ascertain the good or evil in a given situation or when he makes an effort to evaluate the worth of an individual life. Those writers or teachers who are sure of their own system of values or who have committed themselves to a set of religious or philosophical beliefs have, naturally, less difficulty in the assignment of praise or blame to historical figures. Additionally, such people are more positive that history itself contains moral lessons and preachments which only await the discovery and exploration of the historical researcher. The problem of whether or not the historian ought to be a moralist, a compiler of ethical guidelines by which men can judge the past and learn for the present, is as old as Lord Acton for twentieth-century historiography; but, like the making of generalizations of which it is an important part, it has received added urgency as a result of the physical and spiritual crisis of the contemporary world.

In retrospect the role of historical moralist will not be as difficult

[34] Avery Craven, "The Price of Union," *Journal of Southern History*, Vol. XVIII (February, 1952), 3. This is not to say, however, that there has been no dispute over the *techniques* of arriving at generalization. For two distinct views see Thomas C. Cochran, "History and the Social Sciences," in Eisenstadt (ed.), *The Craft of American History*, II, 91, 109; and Trygve Tholfsen, *Historical Thinking: An Introduction*, 276, 279.

for writers of American history to play as it might be for their European counterparts. Beginning with George Bancroft, most of the great American historians have been moralists who have observed in the stream of American history some special set of principles which deserved preservation. They have been, according to David Noble, Jeremiahs warning their countrymen whenever they detected a straying from the path of purity first blazoned through the sinful wilderness by the Puritans.[35] That tradition is still very much with us, and since 1945 its adherents have increased in number.

A classic expression of the tradition was made by Samuel Eliot Morison in a valedictory statement to his colleagues in 1964. Because it contains most of the elements which other historians have emphasized in arguing for the moral function of history, it is quoted here at length:

> As I look back over the years and observe the state of the world today, my last word to my fellow historians is to remind them that they are responsible both to man and to God. They must avoid exacerbating the angry passions of race and nation which threaten to destroy the world; and on the positive side they may help to prove that hate, greed, and pride have been destructive forces in human history. My hope is that some of our younger historians may prove to be instruments by which the brooding dread of our time may be dispelled, and a new and radiant era opened in human history.[36]

This succinct declaration possesses the three basic components which one discovers in varying degrees of emphasis in most other declarations by historians of the postwar period advocating a moral function for history: first, the recognition of the perilous state of world conditions; second, the appeal to a higher authority or law which sets the standard for human conduct (in this case, God); and, finally, the recommendation concerning the way in which historians may help make the world a better and safer place. While it certainly may be argued that the appeal to a Being who has ultimate authority for judging the human situation represents an a priori

---

[35] David W. Noble, *Historians Against History*, 3–4.
[36] Samuel Eliot Morison, *Vistas of History*, 57.

assumption, even those who make no reference to a deity rest their advocacy upon some scheme of ethical behavior which has its origins outside the individual man but is taken as containing generally approved truisms: "hate, greed, and pride have been destructive forces in human history."

Substantiating examples are abundant, although it is perhaps significant that most of them come from that generation of historians who reached maturity during the turbulent days of the thirties and forties. C. H. McIlwain contended that one of the most important jobs of the historian was to distinguish between the permanent and the ephemeral in the human past and "to retain what is good and to reject what is bad." The historian, claimed George Carson, was responsible for keeping alive the principle that "there are values higher than the material or realist approach," and Robert Partin stated that history was the best "measuring stick with which to appraise the bewildering events which swirl around the head of modern man."[37]

The most thoughtful and promising approach to a reinvigoration of the historian as a moral critic was suggested by John Higham in 1962.[38] Though concentrating specifically upon American historiography, his contentions apply equally well to any field of history. Higham traced the moral role of the historian from the nearly absolutist stance of the nineteenth century through the attempt at scientific neutrality to the limited moral pragmatism of the progressive historians and the blurring of moral judgments found in the consensus historians of the postwar period. Arguing that each of these positions was insufficient to the needs of the modern age, he asked that historians cultivate the art of moral insight, which, he

[37] C. H. McIlwain, "The Historian," in R. B. Heywood (ed.), *The Works of the Mind*, 200; George B. Carson, Jr., "The Proper Scope of History," *Western Humanities Review*, Vol. X (Winter, 1955–56), 41; Robert Partin, "The Use of History," *Alabama Review*, Vol. XIX (April, 1966), 119. Other statements along the same lines may be found in Lynn Thorndike, "Whatever Was, Was Right," *American Historical Review*, Vol. LXI (January, 1956), 267; Kenneth S. Latourette, "The Christian Understanding of History," *American Historical Review*, Vol. LIV (January, 1949), 267–68; Read, "The Social Responsibilities of the Historian," *American Historical Review*, Vol. LV (January, 1950), 285.

[38] John Higham, "Beyond Consensus: The Historian as Moral Critic," *American Historical Review*, Vol. LXVII (April, 1962), 609–25.

contended, could be acquired as a professional skill. Then history could be written by historians who were human beings sensitive to the finer qualities of the human spirit. Such history would of necessity subordinate causal interpretation to moral interpretation, but the result would be a more meaningful and dynamic history. Higham discounted the necessity of establishing a system of moral absolutes. "Instead of depending on fixed canons or rules, the moral critic must learn from the great dramatists, like Shakespeare, from novelists, like Tolstoy, and from the matchless example of Thucydides." The historian would use for the task "all the resources of his human condition" and he would uncover in the process "the profoundest struggles and conflicts that the drama of history affords."

Undoubtedly one of those profound struggles was the unceasing campaign of the individual human being and the societies he formed to obtain the maximum amount of freedom. Nineteenth-century historians, giants like Lord Acton in England and Francis Parkman or George Bancroft in America, had detected the struggle for freedom as forming history's master pattern, an undergirding archetype which shaped both individual and national destinies. But their discernment derived largely from the still-acceptable idea of progress which was assumed to be a rather automatic process that historians could take for granted; this was no longer the case in the world of nuclear fission and seemingly endless war. Yet there remained a certain confidence that one of the functions of history was the promotion of human freedom and, furthermore, the belief that a study of history was in itself a liberating process. In 1940 the philosopher Mortimer Adler expressed this sentiment, shared by many of the postwar historians, when he observed that history was an emancipator who freed us from both "the dead hand of tradition and the provincialism of the present moment."[39] It was an understandable hope in the chaos of 1940, and it is even more comprehensible in the postwar era. By itself, however, Adler's declaration and others similar to it take on the aspect of a Pollyanna homily; often repeated as verities of the profession, they lose much of their believability in

[39] Mortimer J. Adler, "Docility and History," *Commonweal*, Vol. XXXII (April 26, 1940), 7.

the retelling, and their truth often seems belied by the appalling nature of the world scene. But there is a more subtle character to the affirmation that history demonstrates liberty which has been prominent in pronouncements about the historical function: the notion that a careful examination of history reveals the free agency of human actors. This belief, while avoiding the confines of any structural determinism, at the same time removes the comfort which such boundaries afford and affixes a truly awful responsibility upon the participants within the historical drama. It is history without illusion, stripped bare of artifice and convention; but it is history that offers real hope of helping man to achieve the ancient dream of freedom.[40]

All the various functions for history and historians which have been advocated in the contemporary period have either dimly or vividly perceived the ultimate result as the enhancement of human self-knowledge whether in the individual or in the collective sense. The making of generalizations, the comprehension of the present, even the advancement of the cause of human freedom, all are aimed at an enlightenment of the mind which can both temper and liberate. The ancient belief that the first task of the civilized man is to know himself summarizes very well the viewpoint of thoughtful historians. At the most elemental level this is the reason history is studied and at the highest level is its most lofty rationale. In the words of T. H. Von Laue, history's function is "to sustain the very heartbeat of human purpose."[41]

It is difficult to argue that anything which permits man's capacity to understand himself to expand can be either ignoble or meaningless. The record of the past is too replete with examples of the

40 Two of the best statements concerning the relationship between a study of history and human freedom are to be found in Philip J. Wolfson, "Freidrich Meinecke (1862–1954)," *Journal of the History of Ideas*, Vol. XVII (October, 1956), 525; and in Max Savelle, "Historian's Progress or the Quest for Sancta Sophia," *Pacific Historical Review*, Vol. XXVII (February, 1958), 25. Savelle, however, in the same article registers strong dissent to the idea of the historian as moralist; see pp. 15–17.

41 Sidney Mead, "Church History Explained," *Church History*, Vol. XXVII (March, 1963), 23; Norman Cantor, *Medieval History*, 1–2; Von Laue, "Is There a Crisis in the Writing of History?" *Bucknell Review*, Vol. XLV (December, 1966), 15.

catastrophes which can occur because of the human failure to understand other human needs and aspirations. The greatest irony in all
of history is the remarkable progress which has been achieved in the
mastery of the environment and the superb technological conquests
when paralleled with the unfathomed mysteries which still remain
around the author of all this achievement. History is one method of
getting at these mysteries. Assuredly it is not the only way, but it
still is one of the best tools for looking at the record of man in
something approaching a total view. This does not imply that historians will discover in their study a magic key which will unlock
some as yet unfound golden door; history will certainly reveal the
complexity of man, but it can also "expose the nature of man as
revealed in simpler and more natural conditions, where that which
was elemental was less concealed by artificialities."[42]

The accretion of knowledge about the past does not by itself
guarantee an increased ability to understand ourselves. What is
required is the utilization of that aggregate "by a fusion of imaginative insight and critical inquiry."[43] By sharing vicariously the experiences of others, their terrors and joys, their sureties and doubts,
their longings and frustrations, we expand our own capacities and
also those of society, and in their expansion move, however painfully, closer toward an understanding of the self and the world in
which it lives.[44]

[42] George F. Kennan, "The Experience of Writing History," *Virginia Quarterly
Review*, Vol. XXXVI (Spring, 1960), 214.

[43] R. F. Arragon, "History's Changing Image: With Such Permanence as Time
Has," *American Scholar*, Vol. XXXIII (Spring, 1964), 233.

[44] Excellent statements which demonstrate support for self-knowledge as history's
highest function are found in Lynn White, Jr., "The Social Responsibility of Scholarship: History," *Journal of Higher Education*, Vol. XXXII (October, 1961), 359;
Dexter Perkins, "We Shall Gladly Teach," *American Historical Review*, Vol. LXII
(January, 1957), 300; and Smith, *The Historian and History*, 245.

CHAPTER 4

**The Individual
Among
Historians**

Nothing has so distinguished modern life as the movement toward a mass society. Basically a product of the industrial revolution and its demands for mass markets to absorb an overflowing cornucopia of goods, the mass society was further enlarged by the dramatic changes in transportation and communication which made possible not only a mass market but also a mass audience. The resultant homogenization of goods and services had a definite impact on the way in which entrepeneurs, managers, and manipulators of the system viewed their clients and customers; usually they found it necessary to think and operate in terms of the mass rather than the individual, to search for a common denominator rather than to accept the uniqueness of personality. It was only natural in such a milieu for people to contemplate the world around them in light of the seemingly impersonal forces which governed it. Individual men and their exploits appeared pale and impotent by comparison, and to many it was somehow more comforting to ascribe the evils of the time to giant gray abstractions (nationalism, imperialism, capitalism, communism, and so on) than to attempt to assess any personal liability. A major result of the concern with the mass, the group, and the impenetrable forces created by science and technology was a dehumanization of life which has been one of the primary ingredients of the twentieth-century tragedy.

It is not too much to assert that the depersonalization attendant to the last century has been one of the factors which led to the extermination factories at Auschwitz and Buchenwald, the eradication of the kulaks in Soviet Russia, and to the acceptance of the idea of saturation bombing by the Allies in World War II. These are, of course, the extremes; but a lack of concern for the individual has affected modern life in a number of other and more subtle ways. From the computerization of income tax returns to the utilization of subliminal advertising, the individual encounters at almost every level of existence some attempt to treat him as something other than a distinct and unique personality. Nor has scholarship been immune to the persuasive argument that it is necessary to understand the strange, new forces of the world if there is to be any hope of dealing with them. Most of the social sciences embraced the trend with enthusiasm, having already a predilection in that direction. Preoccupied with group models and delineations, with economic units and statistical summaries, with the psychology of social status or group therapy, sociologists, economists, and psychologists sought to explain society on the basis of forces, factors, and groups. Under such circumstances the individual often became a mere puppet who was pushed in one direction and then pulled in another by alien energies he neither understood nor controlled. History and historians were also forced to accommodate. The impersonality of the world in which they lived, the insistent demands for comprehension of forces, and the importation of scientific historiography from Germany combined to make writers of history in America less and less concerned with the "who" of history and more and more involved with the "whats" and "whys."

The rejection of the literary historians which was part of the larger repudiation of the romantic movement was accompanied in American historical circles by a growing fascination with the possibilities of transforming the writing of history into a science. Incorporating the scientific method and its special German form, the seminar, American colleges and universities followed the precedent of Johns Hopkins, established the doctor of philosophy degree, and concentrated their historical research on institutions rather than men.[1] What had begun primarily as a methodological device soon

[1] The writing of history was not, of course, the only discipline to be affected by a popular scientism. Philosophy had been engaged in vigorous discourse since the time of the French Revolution and its aftermath. Indeed, one of the basic cleavages between philosophers had developed about the significance of the individual. While it is misleading to oversimplify the situation and assign individual thinkers to one camp or the other, it is nevertheless fairly accurate to say that the English and

developed pretensions to something more—to attain the substance as well as the technique of science. If history were to imitate successfully chemistry, physics, and biology, then it would have to adopt the main characteristic of those disciplines; Clio must become predictive; it must discover laws which were universal in their application. The labors of Henry Adams and his brother Brooks Adams are the most illustrative examples of this tendency.[2] The only predictable result from the effort to achieve a quality of prediction was that such attempts were foredoomed to failure, for, as A. M. Taylor has reminded historians: "The human equation in history forever bans its data from the realm of strict experimental science, and makes its interpretation necessarily subjective and psychological."[3] Nevertheless, a shift in emphasis occurred which had significant effects on the writing of history for fifty years. This was the transfer of historical attention from the personal to the impersonal. Although in many ways the new emphasis was a necessary corrective, the role of the individual upon history's stage was relegated far too often to a second-act walk-on, serving only to advance the plot rather than to be its focus.

The concepts of the "new history" popularized in the academic world by James Harvey Robinson and others did nothing to reverse the trend away from serious consideration of the individual personality. True, Robinson and his supporters objected to some of the canons of scientific historiography, principally the latter's dedication

---

French romantics were more convinced of the import of the individual than were the German idealists. Especially pertinent for later developments in historiography was the historical philosophy of Georg W. F. Hegel, who elaborated a thesis of history as spirit or idea which to a large degree denigrated the impact of the individual while exalting the value of the group, particularly the state. Nineteenth-century philosophical currents were a most important part of the ideological foundation for scientific history.

2 For an interesting and enlightening study of the relationship of German thought to American historians see Jurgen Herbst, *The German Historical School in American Scholarship*, especially Chap. 5. I examined the search made by the Adams brothers for historical laws in *Henry Adams and Brooks Adams: The Education of Two American Historians.*

3 A. M. Taylor, "A Vitalistic Philosophy of History," *Journal of Social Philosophy*, Vol. VI (January, 1941), 138.

to the idea of pristine objectivity and its attitude of detachment from the contemporary world; but the major thrust of the critics was aimed at the narrowness in scope of the traditional history. More than anything else, the devotees of the "new history" wanted to broaden both the content and function of history. They were convinced of the importance of social, economic, cultural, and intellectual history and believed that these areas had long been neglected in preference for the more traditional work in political, constitutional, and military history. Furthermore, their advocacy of a more inclusive historiography was directly related to their belief in history as reform tool.[4] But they did not resurrect the study of the individual. Seeing history as largely the history of groups and ideas as convenient abstractions, the "new history" was often "more scientific than 'scientific' history itself," insisting that "the historian must apply the scientific method of subsuming materials under general concepts and of mastering them thereby."[5]

The introduction of relativist theory into historical speculation did much in the twenties and thirties to destroy the myth of certitude which cloaked scientific history, but it did little to enhance the position of the individual within the historical process. Carl Becker and Charles Beard precipitated many battles between generations of historians, brought about a searching re-examination of many of the profession's most sacred tenets, and caused a philosophical crisis of some magnitude for the nation's more thoughtful scholars, but they largely avoided the problem of the individual. They were more concerned with the impact that the historian himself exercised upon the way in which history was written and presented than they were with the significance of the historical figure upon the actual movement of history. Indeed, in many instances relativism contributed to the problem. If the past was given additional mystery because of its unknowability, how much more unfathomable were those shadowy people who inhabited it. Understanding the individual human being

4 Some excellent comments on the viewpoint of the "new history" may be found in Higham, "The Rise of American Intellectual History," *American Historical Review*, Vol. LVI (April, 1951), 458.

5 Lloyd R. Sorenson, "Charles A. Beard and German Historiography," *Mississippi Valley Historical Review*, Vol. XLII (September, 1955), 275.

had always been the most difficult of tasks. Was it not even more difficult when the student could no longer trust the completeness of his records, the evidence of witnesses, or, finally, himself? When the relativists claimed that the historian was unable to divorce his research from his own set of biases and beliefs or to compensate for his own contemporaneity, they were making the dilemma of comprehending the individual in history that much more insoluble. Or so it seemed. On the eve of World War II historians had traveled a road which had led from the formalism of scientific certainty to the formlessness of relativistic uncertainty. As has already been observed, however, the war was to act as a catalyst for historical study, and one of the results was a revolt against the depersonalization of history and a revival of interest in the individual.

The rebellion against the dehumanization of existence affected many more facets of the intellectual community than just the writing of history. In fact, the movement permeated popular culture as well, and its expression could be noted in various ways: in distinct and different clothing fashions, in the decline in regular political party affiliation in preference for an independent status, in the struggle for civil rights by black America with its stress upon the integrity of the individual, in the growing popularity of abstraction in art which placed such strong emphasis upon individual interpretation, and in myriad other ways. People naturally objected to being catalogued and stereotyped, to being automatically computerized into this or that group. They instinctively recognized that there was something degrading and less than human in the process, and they sought methods in which they might express more vividly their own uniqueness. Historians were themselves a part of this larger scene, but, perhaps along with those pursuing the other humane studies, they felt more keenly than most the threat which an indifference to the individual posed. In a very serious way the trend threatened the life of history as a humanity and forced historians to come to grips with basic philosophical questions. While the questions were nearly as old as history itself, the need for answers had never been more compelling.

That historians should be more directly concerned with the individual man was emphasized by philosophers of history as well as historians and undoubtedly was an influential contributing factor in the movement to refocus attention upon personality. Shortly before the end of World War II, Paul Weiss stated that "men turn to history primarily to learn three truths—how men have changed, what makes men change, and what men are, despite all change."[6] Indirectly he was pointing the historian in the direction of his audience where the final decision about the relevance of history to society is made. Implicit within Weiss's statement was an acknowledgement that forces or factors, or "change," as he termed it, was within the framework of appropriate study but that it was of interest only inasmuch as it affected the individual. And there was the assumption that, however man and his life were manipulated, something, some inner core, remained constant. "What men are"—that was the central subject. The historian, by telling man what he had been in terms that were meaningful to modern man, with his own set of paradoxes, ambivalences, and doubts, could assist in informing man of what he was and even, perhaps, of what he might become.

Another philosopher, Charles Frankel, likewise has stressed the necessity for explaining the "meaning of events in terms of the actual, private, short-term values." Asserting that "history does not go on only behind men's backs; it also goes on under their skins," Frankel warned historians of the pitfall of meaninglessness awaiting to entrap those "who can see only the embracing pattern of events."[7] History had to recapture its ability to record the past in a manner which ensnared the quality of human universality and demonstrated the commonality among men of all ages and times. It had been the realization of this truism that had knit together Western society along with a belief in the absolute uniqueness of the individual. Paradoxical as it might appear, a major facet of Western thought was the actuality of this relationship: similarity and dissimilarity contained within both the individual and his history. This was not unfamiliar ground

[6] Paul Weiss, "History and the Historian," *Journal of Philosophy*, Vol. XLII (March 29, 1945), 177.

[7] Charles Frankel, "Philosophy and History," *Political Science Quarterly*, Vol. LXXII (September, 1957), 368–69.

for the historian as he had always been made by the nature of his craft to consider both the particular and the general. What was feared by many writers of history was that the emphasis had shifted too far in the direction of the general, and that unless a readjustment was effected the broad humanizing role played by the historian as the traditional explicator of the past to the present might well atrophy. To counteract this trend historians since 1945 have formulated general statements of principle and have also examined other and more complicating aspects of the problem, including the questions of human freedom, the totality of human personality, individual uniqueness, and the matter of irrationality.

The fear that historians had lost sight of the individual was best expressed by Carl Bridenbaugh in his presidential address to the American Historical Association in 1962. Because of its summary qualities and its challenging character it deserves quotation at length:

> We historians appear to have lost our former realization of the historical importance of the individual, of the human being. We discourse learnedly of peasants in the mass, as a class, as though each one did not possess an individuality and reveal the eccentricities we note immediately as we look at the paintings of Brueghel. "History is about chaps," the English tell us; yet neither they nor we seem able to remember that chaps still belong in written history. They are the most important part of it—the hard core, if I may coin a phrase.[8]

Bridenbaugh went on to criticize the growing fascination of historians with the methods of the social sciences, declaring that "the finest historians will not be those who succumb to the dehumanizing methods of social sciences, whatever their uses and values, which I hasten to acknowledge." Future historians, he warned, "will have to acquire, and it will call out their utmost efforts, . . . a sense of individual men living and having their daily being, men acting in time and place, or there will be no comprehension."[9]

Bridenbaugh's feeling that there was danger to the historian in refusing to spend more of his energies on an understanding of the

8 Carl Bridenbaugh, "The Great Mutation," *American Historical Review*, Vol. LXVIII (January, 1963), 323.
9 *Ibid.*, 326–27.

individual stemmed largely from his belief that a primary goal of history was its broadening role in the educational process. Moreover, history which dealt only with groups and forces assumed the risk of becoming something other than history. As Louis Gottschalk stated, "The historian is distinguished from other scholars most markedly by the emphasis he places upon the role of individual motives, actions, accomplishments, failures, and contingencies in historical continuity and change." To forget or ignore the basic element of individual human aspiration, action, and motivation was to most historians to forget the very nature of the craft and to misplace emphasis at a time when the enigma of personality was more than ever in need of understanding. Man was being asked in the present age by the critical and cataclysmic events swirling around him to know himself in order that he might exercise some control over his destiny. Only the humanistic tradition with its historical foundation could supply the necessary insights, the broad base of knowledge. This structure, suggested Julian Boyd, is the one "upon which we must ultimately rely if life in this new world is to be worth living."[10]

Most consistently repeated among the proponents of individualized history was the theme immortalized by Alexander Pope in that famous couplet which ends with the admonition that the proper study of mankind is man. Subtract man from the historical equation and it becomes meaningless, because, many insisted, history is written for man. R. M. Morse, writing in the *Political Science Quarterly*, admitted that man might not be "the most important thing in the universe" but argued that he must be the "core of history" because "to *us* man is the most important thing." In his criticism of the Social Science Research Council *Bulletin 64*, James C. Malin contended that in omitting consideration of the individual and dealing only in abstraction the report had produced "purely subjective constructs that possess no reality except in the mind." Jennings

[10] Gottschalk, "A Professor of History in a Quandary," *American Historical Review*, Vol. LIX (January, 1954), 279; Julian P. Boyd, "A Modest Proposal to Meet an Urgent Need," *American Historical Review*, Vol. LXX (January, 1965), 342.

Sanders maintained that it is only because "man is central in history that historical studies are at once exciting, challenging, and perplexing."[11] The viewpoint was best capsulized by Philip Davidson who predicted that

> we can and will have scholars of broader interests and greater humanistic fervor who will neither be indifferent to history in its broader aspects, nor doubt that the proper study of history is man, and that the proper study of man involves history.[12]

Interwoven in the Davidson statement are the twin ideas which form the substantive arguments supporting the contention that history must be concerned with the problem of the individual. The first of these, the notion that the proper study of history is man, is essentially objective in that it sees as the object units of historical study individual human beings acting within the context of time and space. The historian thus concentrates upon definable, if bewildering, entities. The records which are the sources of all his information have been produced by individual men. He cannot divorce his documents from their creators without producing an artificial situation that is at once unreal and misleading. This is not to say that human beings are the only reality, only that they are the only reality for which the historian has any special competence. History may well reveal that men are often moved by forces over which they exercise no individual control, but the task of the historian is not so much to delineate and explain the forces as it is to demonstrate their effects on men.

The second idea emphasizes the subjective aspect. For whom is history written? Obviously, it is written for men to read—not as a

11 R. M. Morse, "The Modern Scholar and the Americas," *Political Science Quarterly*, Vol. LXV (December, 1950), 524–25; James C. Malin, *The Contriving Brain and the Skillful Hand in the United States*, 370. Jennings Sanders, *Historical Interpretations and American Historianship*, 21–22. A statement by Richard L. Watson in discussing the writing of political history captured the basic concept by acknowledging "the indispensable human factor without which history is comparatively simple to write, but meaningless." See "American Political History," *South Atlantic Quarterly*, Vol. LIV (January, 1955), 108.

12 Philip Davidson, review of Loren C. McKinney (ed.), *A State University Surveys the Humanities*, in *Mississippi Valley Historical Review*, Vol. XXXIII (March, 1947), 640.

product being forced upon an unwilling audience but as one which fulfills a recognizable human need. It is what history can do for the individual that makes it important.[13] The individual as the stuff of history and the individual as the user of history is the duality which always confronts the historian and which he ignores at the peril of obsolescence.

The most compelling and persuasive arguments on behalf of the significance of the individual within history have been constructed around the rationale of antideterminism. Many historians have reflected the discontent of other intellectuals with any system which deprives the individual of personal option in the decision-making processes of his own life or those of his society. Undertones of the ancient philosophical dilemma between free will and predestination were present, but it would be a mistake to assume that they formed the core of discussion. Historians were less concerned with arguing from either theological or philosophical bases than they were in speaking from their own experiences as students of history. The historical record seemed to contain enough examples and illustrations to make a very strong case for the openness of history.

For some a history which emphasized the general (groups, movements, eras, forces) at the expense of the particular was guilty of advancing the notion of closed determinism, of seeing history as mechanism, and of an abstractionism which perverted the multiplicity of history. Arthur Schlesinger, Jr., has commented that, "for the working historian . . . , there is no escape from the interpretation of history by individuals in terms of the purposes and characters of other individuals," and he rejected the idea that history could "be contained in a single interpretation or seen from a single perspective." It was the danger of monism which disturbed the historian when he encountered preoccupation with forces or groups. One of the chief contributions of Arnold J. Toynbee to historiography, according to Richard E. Sullivan, has been the stress he has placed upon the human factor. Toynbee "ought at least to make historians

13 Hajo Holborn, "History and the Humanities," *Journal of the History of Ideas,* Vol. IX (January, 1948), 65–69.

skeptical of their tendency to support determinism." When the historian tries to impose pattern or structure upon history, the temptation is always present to see the same pattern over and over. These patterns, Howard M. Smyth has reminded us, "are abstractions which acquire historical value only when they animate or inspire living men."[14]

The whole problem of individual freedom in history is closely related to the question of historical inevitability, for if events move toward an undisclosed but unchangeable end, then it is futile to speak of option and choice for the individual. It is also true that the very nomenclature employed by historians often lends itself to the assumption of inevitability; words like "cause," "result," and "factor" carry with them the connotation of impersonal force traveling toward an already determined point in time. Because historians deal with what did happen as opposed to what might have happened, their narratives frequently read as though one event followed another in a locked sequence.

Historians are also prisoners of what might be called "future knowledge"; for example, it is practically impossible for one to write of eighteenth-century France without remembering that in 1789 the *ancien régime* crumpled in revolution. It is equally difficult for American historians to record the history of the 1850's without pointing things toward the clash which began at Fort Sumter in April, 1861. There is a natural tendency to search for those matters which contribute to the known outcome and to overlook items which do not conform. Frequently forgotten is the fact that in any given historical situation the individual actors were confronted with a series of alternatives. That they selected one option over another does not prove that it was the only one available or considered. When viewed within the context of his own personal experience, the historian recognizes the truth of this proposition, and, as Arthur Bestor maintains, "The historian cannot project into the past a

14 Arthur M. Schlesinger, Jr., "The Thread of History: Freedom or Fatality?" *Reporter*, Vol. XIII (December 15, 1955), 47; Sullivan, "Toynbee's Debtors," *South Atlantic Quarterly*, Vol. LVII (Winter, 1959), 86–87; Howard M. Smyth, review of Federico Chabod, *Storia Della Politica Estera Italiana Dal 1870 Al 1896*, in *American Historical Review*, Vol. LVII (July, 1952), 973.

greater determinism than he (and his fellowmen) can discover in their own personal lives."[15]

In the postwar period historians in the United States have consistently stressed the significance of alternatives available to individuals in historical situations. The strongest statement has probably been made by Page Smith, who insisted that "if we see history more truly as the creation of man's effective will and action—and this is what historical investigation shows it to be—we can find the heart, . . . to act as men." Additionally, Smith avowed that process and behavior are "always subordinate to intelligent and purposeful action." Garrett Mattingly, complaining that social scientists tend to forget the difference between mice and men, declared that the distinguishing characteristic of history is that men have alternatives, while Max Savelle has said that "nothing is inevitable in history except the flow of history itself" and that "men, by taking thought, may control the direction of the flow."[16] Both Savelle and Bradford Smith believed that an important part of the problem originated in the blindness that results when group actions are not seen as a collection of individual actions.[17] Abstractions are human inventions; only the individual human being is alive.

The simple assertion, however, that the individual was free did not necessarily make him so, nor did it eliminate force as a factor in human history. It was obvious that the individual was never totally free, that he was subject to many forces over which he could exercise no direct control. His freedom, then, was contained as much in his ability to respond in various ways to his own situation as it was in his power to initiate action. It was this freedom, the tension between

15 Bestor, "The Humaneness of History," in Eisenstadt, (ed.), *The Craft of American History*, I, 14.

16 Smith, *The Historian and History*, 213; Garrett Mattingly, "The Use of History," *Atlantic*, Vol. CLXXVII (July, 1946), 124–28; Max Savelle, "Historian's Progress, or, The Quest for Sancta Sophia," *Pacific Historical Review*, Vol. XXVII (February, 1958), 18.

17 Max Savelle, "The Function of History in the Age of Science," *Historian*, Vol. XXII (August, 1960), 359; Bradford Smith, "Biographer's Creed," *William and Mary Quarterly*, 3d Series, Vol. X (April, 1953), 194. See also the statement by Boyd C. Shafer, "Men Are More Alike," *American Historical Review*, Vol. LVII (April, 1952), 594.

personality and environment, that prompted historians to reject any rigid determinism. The crucial point, said Oscar Handlin, is the point of interaction between the individual and social forces "where a man's destiny affects his times." Moreover, the individual may be subjected to a multiplicity of forces, which are, at best, difficult to identify as to degree of strength and influence. Most would agree with Trygve Tholfsen that the historian "cannot take refuge in a theory of absolute freedom or rigid determinism" but "must look carefully into the role of the individual, who is never the mere puppet of impersonal forces."[18]

Undoubtedly the large deprivations of individual freedom occurring in the present century and justified by schemes of historical determinism have had great influence in shaping the affirmations of individual importance made by historians, especially historians in America, where the traditional faith in democracy was particularly hospitable to ideas positing the worth and dignity of the individual. The rejection of the notion of the closed society was in keeping with that tradition, but it was more than that, more than a matter of national ideas; it was a matter also of professional self-preservation, for, unless history was indeed open, its movement dictated largely by the actions of individual human agents, then the role of the historian was reduced to that of technician and graph plotter rather than that of perceptive humanist whose labors offered inspiration and hope for the future. Most preferred to believe with Hans Kohn that:

> History rightly studied can sharpen man's critical insight into human relationships and personality; it makes him more conscious of his limitations and therefore more humble but also teaches him to regard the future as open.[19]

[18] Oscar Handlin, "The History in Men's Lives," *Virginia Quarterly Review*, Vol. XXX (Summer, 1954), 541; Tholfsen, *Historical Thinking: An Introduction*, 284.

[19] Kohn, "A Historian's Creed for Our Time," *South Atlantic Quarterly*, Vol. LII (July, 1953), 343. Other comments which make essentially the same point may be found in Walter L. Dorn, "Personality and History," *Journal of Higher Education*, Vol. XXXIII (January, 1962), 20–29; and in Donald M. Dozer, "History as Force," *Pacific Historical Review*, Vol. XXXIV (November, 1965), 388. See also

Despite the general affirmation given to the significance of the individual by postwar historians, the very complex problem of explaining and evaluating him remained. Nothing seems as enigmatic as personality, as incapable of certainty, as deceptive when judgment is based upon surface actions. The student of history could not allow himself to be seduced by mere words or even actions into believing that with these manifestations he really understood the mystery inherent in the individual personality. Those forces and wellsprings which produced a certain human action were often hidden deep within the human psyche, as often as not from the actor himself. Yet it was apparent that, for even partial comprehension, the inner life of the individual must be penetrated, its remoter regions explored, and its basic elements uncovered. How the individual felt and thought were as important in acquiring understanding as were his words and his actions. Indeed, only by knowing the former could the latter be rendered intelligible.

History, said Trygve Tholfsen, came to be based on a new understanding of man with the writings of Johann Gottfried Herder, who brought to attention human individuality and the value of studying people as totalities. Historians who failed to go deeper than the outer manifestations of personality were incapable of conquering the difficult problems of motivation and historical causation. To Tholfsen, "Events are but the outer expression of the inner life of the soul, and the historian must penetrate to that inner reality." To accomplish this task, two methods have been suggested, both of which involve introspective acts on the part of the historian, as well as a continuation of the more traditional examination of the documents germane to his study. The first of these methods would simply formalize a device which many writers of history have frequently employed in the past, namely, the development of the quality of historical-mindedness to the point that the writer is able to achieve an empathy with those whom he is portraying. This approach does not imply approval of the writer's subjects or their actions, but it does denote an understanding of those subjects, their times, and

Walter B. Rundell, Jr., "History Teaching: A Legitimate Concern," *Social Education*, Vol. XXIX (December, 1965), 524.

their reasons for acting as they did. There is the natural danger that empathy can lead to an apologia. This danger is something against which the historian must constantly guard, but it need not be an insuperable obstacle to a clear and accurate presentation. In commenting on voting behavior and patterns, Samuel P. Hays has said that "we have to examine what people feel and think and experience, and see their political action as a product of those inner events." In short, the historian must put himself in the times and skins of his characters. Second, the historian may be able to comprehend the individuals he finds in history by looking inside himself and weighing his own experiences. The thoughtful person realizes the large complexity which is himself and understands that the actions he takes and the words he utters are not simple expressions traceable to a single cause rooted always in rationality but are the products of a fabric whose strands are multifaceted and whose ultimate source is often hidden. Inner meditation of this sort may not always arrive at the truth, but it is still a trustworthy method, for its practitioner will know "how blended are dust and fire in the innermost recesses of the human heart."[20]

While the above devices are no guarantee of historical certitude, the historian who uses them will discover at least one truth: the uniqueness of every individual. He may also find areas of commonality, but the most striking aspect of his researches will be the knowledge that each individual must be accepted and explained on the basis of his own singularity. If historians are wise, intimates August C. Krey, they will know in addition that, "however important these common characteristics may be, the dynamic quality of society is derived from the individuals who set the mass in motion or determine its direction and are therefore distinctive." This insight into the nature of history is the more remarkable for being so often overlooked; the temptation to see only the pattern within a group can be overwhelming. Yet, without the leaven of an irreducible individuality, written history remains a gray serving of neutral substance

[20] Tholfsen, *Historical Thinking: An Introduction*, 136; Samuel P. Hays, "History as Human Behavior," in Eisenstadt (ed.), *The Craft of American History*, II, 131; Bestor, "The Humaneness of History," *ibid.*, I, 15.

devoid of life because it lacks life's most essential component—the individual human being. Lloyd Sorenson predicted that in the history yet to be written "distinctiveness, unrepeatability, radical individuality will come to be considered the most vital aspects of historical objects." The kind of knowledge which will accrue from such efforts will not be comparable to that accumulated by science, but it will be human knowledge, the kind that history at its very best has always offered to mankind, the kind described by Arthur Bestor as "knowledge about beings infinitely various, unpredictably brave and unpredictably cowardly, successful in their designs at one time, unsuccessful at another."[21]

The longer the historian ponders the wide variety of individual personalities the more he becomes convinced that a proper evaluation must rest upon an ability to see the total human being, each seen within a particular context of time and space. Comparison and contrast of individuals with others may be revealing and helpful, but they will never comprise a completely satisfactory answer to the riddle of human motivation and action. One can learn something about the tactics and strategies of would-be conquerors by comparing Napoleon with Alexander the Great, Louis XIV, and Adolph Hitler, and such information will be both valid and useful. That it will also give the student greater knowledge of Napoleon the man is doubtful, for the French emperor was the product of a background and times which were peculiar to him alone. What he did in any given situation brought into play all that he was and all that he had felt and experienced. It is possible to admit that human nature has fundamental constants within it without also making the assumption that such seeming eternals as love, hate, greed, and status are always present in the same degree or in the same combination.[22] W. B.

[21] August C. Krey, *History and the Social Web*, 205–206; Lloyd R. Sorenson, "Historical Currents in America," *American Quarterly*, Vol. VII (Fall, 1955), 246; Bestor, "The Humaneness of History," in Eisenstadt (ed.), *The Craft of American History*, I, 13.

[22] Two thoughtful discussions of the significance of human nature for the historian are Robert L. Schuyler, "John Richard Green and His Short History," *Political Science Quarterly*, Vol. LXIV (September, 1949), 325–26; and Helmut Kuhn, "Dialectic in History," *Journal of the History of Ideas*, Vol. X (January, 1949), 29.

Willcox has observed that "the whole person is involved in whatever he does" and that the historian must rely to some degree on imagination, since the totality of experience for which he strives is unobtainable. However, historians have agreed in the postwar era that totality should be the goal. To see people as they really are—that is the proper ambition. Page Smith claimed that when the Hebrew writers wrote history, "enacted by real people, with all their faults and blemishes," they "had discovered one of the most essential elements of history." The historian must involve himself, warned Sidney Ratner, in the whole complex of forces and factors which condition the individual. For William A. Williams both the function and the test of the historian was to deal with people as people.[23]

The most perplexing problem facing the historian who wishes to view the human characters of history in their entirety has been that of assigning significance to the role of the irrational in affecting individual motivation. Brought to public notice by the popularization of the studies of Sigmund Freud in the decade of the 1920's and quickly assimilated by novelists like Sherwood Anderson and dramatists like Eugene O'Neill, the ideas of infant sexuality, dreams as wish fulfillment, and other Freudian tools for unlocking the unconscious became common conceits and the conversation topic for countless cocktail parties. To be psychoanalyzed was to be fashionable, and the glib, often ribald, aura which encompassed the subject made most historians wary of using psychoanalytic approaches in their investigations. Indeed, it has only been in comparatively recent times that those historians eager to probe more deeply the sources of human motivation have begun to consider the advisability of exploring the unconscious mind as a legitimate method of discerning some of the whys of human conduct. In 1957, William L. Langer, in a presidential address to the American Historical Association, recommended to his colleagues that their "next assignment" ought to be

23 W. B. Willcox, "An Historian Looks at Social Change," in Eisenstadt (ed.), *The Craft of American History*, I, 17, 33; Smith, *The Historian and History*, 6; Sidney Ratner, "The Historian's Approach to Psychology," *Journal of the History of Ideas*, Vol. II (January, 1941), 95–101; William A. Williams, "The Age of Re-Forming History," *Nation*, June 30, 1956, p. 554.

the employment of techniques and insights borrowed from the psychiatrist. Confessing that it was improbable that the historian would ever have enough evidence to make his representation complete, Langer nevertheless believed that it "is our responsibility, as historians, to leave none of these possibilities unexplored."[24] Richard Hofstadter and Henry Nash Smith were two writers whose work especially recognized the influence of the irrational upon human behavior;[25] only short tentative steps have been taken in this direction, however, and the degree to which the nonrational impulses condition the individual in history has remained largely uncharted and a persistent challenge to the historian who would know better the sources of motivation.

Not all historians have approved the prevailing trend of redirecting attention to the individual and his activities. Objections customarily have fallen into two classifications: one stressing the negative aspect, namely, that the insufficiency of records dealing with personalities prevents the historian from ever arriving at a total evaluation; the other, a more positive complaint, that emphasis upon the individual is misplaced and should more properly be directed toward group experiences and social forces. Martin Duberman believed that the historian can describe "the external world of action" but that the factors underlying behavior are "largely closed to historical investigation." Thomas C. Cochran, long a champion of the applicability of the methods of social science to history, contended that the data about personality were too fragmentary to be of substantial benefit, and Folke Dovring, while not denying the significance of the individual in history, declared that "there cannot be any complete explanation of events where personalities play a role."[26]

[24] William L. Langer, "The Next Assignment," *American Historical Review*, Vol. LXIII (January, 1958), 302–303.

[25] Smith and Hofstadter share the credit "for introducing into professional historical scholarship a large, effective grasp of the non-rational elements in human conduct." Higham in Higham *et al., History,* 229.

[26] Duberman, "The Limitations of History," *Antioch Review*, Vol. XXV (Summer, 1965), 285; Thomas C. Cochran, "History and the Social Sciences," in Eisenstadt (ed.), *The Craft of American History*, II, 109; Dovring, *History as a Social Science*, 68.

Both C. Vann Woodward and David Potter, who have written extensively on the history of the American South and the Civil War, have maintained that the appropriate sphere of historical investigation is the group and its experiences. Potter has stated that, although the historian is concerned with human beings, "he does not deal with them primarily as individuals . . . . Instead he deals with them in groups." Woodward would leave much private experience to the psychologist. "The historian," he said, "is more properly concerned with the public and external forces that go to make up the collective experience and give shape to the group character of a people."[27]

Among many of the historians writing since 1945 there was the feeling that the greater peril to a vital historiography lay in a continuation of the trend toward scientific impersonality which had so characterized the profession in the first forty years of the twentieth century. The danger, warned George B. Carson, was that the individual was being lost. The proper scope of history, he declared, was "to preserve the value of the individual, to preserve the heritage of the human race in which the individual has been more important than the abstraction."[28] Furthermore it was feared that the historian risked an increased dwindling of his audience unless he provided information which was more relevant to individual human experience and more sustaining of human values.[29] In returning to the individual as his central object of concern and concentration, the historian sought to reclaim a lost heritage and to become a more dynamic force in the intellectual commitments of his own age.

[27] David M. Potter, "The Historian's Use of Nationalism and Vice Versa," *American Historical Review*, Vol. LXVII (July, 1962), 924; Woodward, *The Burden of Southern History*, ix.

[28] Carson, "The Proper Scope of History," *Western Humanities Review*, Vol. X (Winter, 1955–56), 39.

[29] This theme is more fully developed in Hays, "History as Human Behavior," in Eisenstadt (ed.), *The Craft of American History*, II, 127; Lewis M. Terman, "Should the Historian Study Psychology?" *Pacific Historical Review*, Vol. X (June, 1941), 212; Frederick H. Cramer, "In Quest of Meaning," *Current History*, New Series, Vol. XIII (July, 1947), 5.

CHAPTER 5

**Causality:
Continuity
and Contingency**

One of the concerns of their age which engaged the attention of
historians during the postwar years was the long-discussed problem
of causality in human history. To historians aware of how central
this question had been to historiographical disputations of the past,
the renewal of discussion seemed often a tedious rehash of questions
and answers for which there was no possibility of discovering solutions. Even to those writers and students of history who were unfamiliar with the rhetoric of past debates, the new contemporary
dialogues must have appeared recognizable because anyone who
has worked at the historian's craft has had to face, either consciously
or unconsciously, the matter of causation and has had to devise his
own formula for satisfying its demands. Most practicing historians
preferred, however, to leave the complexities of causation to philosophers and philosophers of history, who in recent years have written
a good deal about the subject. But in an age when the pressures
generated by history appeared so immediately threatening, the question people most frequently asked of historians was, Why? What had
caused it all? And if the question of causation was of more immediate
import for the historian of the twentieth century, it was nonetheless
of equal significance for all other historians. What was pertinent in
discerning causation for the great movements of modern history
might also be applicable to events in the remoter past. Once again,
though reluctantly, historians were compelled to undertake an examination of what made things happen in history and in the process to
arrive at a clearer understanding of their own capabilities and
limitations.

Aside from the general philosophical question whether it was
possible to know anything concerning past events in the same way

in which the scientist is able to elicit "facts" from his research or to be able to deduce causal relationships from the very sequence of events, historians were forced to re-examine the entire problem of causation from the vantage point of the working historian. It was impossible to deny that the historian in his writing dealt consistently with the problem. The materials he selected to become a part of "his" history, the ordering he gave to those materials, the employment of such words as "consequently," "therefore," "because," "accordingly," and "since," the talk of such things as forces and factors—all testified how much causation was a part of the work of the historian. Yet, despite the commonplace manner in which most writers of history disposed of the problem, very serious and important decisions had to be made before the historian could make any statement why something either had or had not happened.

It was in this decision-making process that the historian came to grips with the essentials of the causative problem. His greatest assets were his training in historical method and his humility before the complexities of the past. Indeed, what has distinguished the professional historian from the amateur has been the awareness of the former that whatever answers he gave to historical questions were likely to be both tentative and subject to later revision. The foremost dilemma encountered in determining causation has been the natural human tendency to ignore multiplicity and seek the comfort of the single answer or formula. On this matter historians since 1945 have been in nearly unanimous agreement. The English historian John Cairns summarized it well: "In the end Clio has no answer, but only answers."[1]

Somewhat ironically, the discernment of the pluralism inherent in historical causation was best adumbrated a decade apart by two gifted historical amateurs, Raymond Gram Swing, the popular liberal newspaper columnist and radio commentator during the turbulent thirties and forties, and George F. Kennan, the Department of State expert on the Soviet Union and author of the containment policy of the Truman era.[2] Writing in 1950, Swing was appalled by

1 John C. Cairns, "Clio and the Queen's First Minister," *South Atlantic Quarterly,* Vol. LII (October, 1953), 519.

the obscurity of knowledge concerning the motivation behind any single action in history. The thoughtful historian was forced into a realization of his own ignorance: "The more one contemplates the innumerable turnings of the road not taken and the inscrutable forces at work in avoiding taking them the less didactic one will be about history having a discernible causation." Ten years later Kennan confessed to similar bewilderment when confronted with the "hopeless open-endedness of the subject of history itself. . . . I was soon brought to realize that every beginning and ending of every historical work is always in some degree artificial and contrived."[3]

Professional historians, less dismayed by both the philosophic and the methodological implications of multiple causation, since it was an ever-present concern in their daily labors, also wrote frequently about the pluralistic nature of history and its inner dynamics. Most noted that the pluralism of history not only characterized the matter of causation but also was applicable to the broad spectrum of historical study. There were as many kinds of history as there were historians. And, rather than spend time in futile protest, the historian should embrace the variety he discovered there. "History," insisted Allan Nevins, "is a house of many mansions." Social and cultural history for example, was "a field in which the village, the provincial town, and the state capital are as important as Washington or London." With the area of historical study itself constantly enlarging, how was it possible to reach any other conclusion about causation than that it too was to be understood only in terms of causes—not a cause? Robert L. Schuyler was most definite: "Causation in history is always multiple, and to single out any one antecedent as a *fundamental* cause is a highly subjective operation. . . . The historian ought, I submit, to banish 'fundamental' causes from his vocabulary." Max Savelle was equally adamant: "There is no single identi-

2 No denigration is intended in describing either Swing or Kennan as amateurs. The use of the word is employed only to indicate that the writing of history was not the original vocation of either man. Certainly no apologies need to be given for Kennan, whose historical works are of the highest merit.

3 Raymond G. Swing, "Is History Bunk?" *Saturday Review of Literature*, Vol. XXXIII (June 3, 1950), 6; Kennan, "The Experience of Writing History," *Virginia Quarterly Review*, Vol. XXXVI (Spring, 1960), 205.

fiable cause of any event or course of events." And in two important articles concerning the problem of causation and the American Civil War, both Lee Benson and Cushing Strout recognized the subjective nature of determining causation and its subsequent multiplicity.[4]

Taking the existence of multiple causation in history for granted, historians additionally argued that their colleagues should adopt, self-consciously, the plural approach in their studies. Far from being a matter over which to despair, such an approach afforded the historian the opportunity to approximate perhaps more closely than any other researcher the reality of the human condition and to make his work meaningful and vital to the contemporary world. John Higham contended that, "to move freely through the complex web of human experience, historians need to employ simultaneously a multitude of causal hypotheses." Echoing the same thought, Harvey Wish stated that "a close view of any complex or controversial historical subject reveals the infinite variety of human responses which cannot be wholly contained in one formula," which, Wish felt, demonstrated the need for "a self-critical approach and for an independent will." From the vantage point of the biographer as well as the historian John Garraty advised the former category to "avoid any oversimplified theory of historical development. The individual makes history; so does chance; so do social forces." The prevailing opinion of historians, therefore, seemed to advocate both the recognition of history's pluralism and the necessity of utilizing a many-faceted approach in its study, enabling the historian to become that synthesizer of knowledge urged on the profession by Trygve Tholfsen.[5]

[4] Allan Nevins, "History This Side the Horizon," in Eisenstadt (ed.), *The Craft of American History*, II, 267; Robert L. Schuyler, "Contingency in History," *Political Science Quarterly*, Vol. LXXIV (September, 1959), 329–30; Savelle, "Historian's Progress, or, The Quest for Sancta Sophia," *Pacific Historical Review*, Vol. XXVII (February, 1958), 18; Lee Benson and Cushing Strout, "Causation and the American Civil War: Two Appraisals," *History and Theory*, Vol. I, No. II (1961), 163–85.

[5] Higham in Higham *et al., History*, 147; Harvey Wish, "The American Historian and the New Conservatism," *South Atlantic Quarterly*, Vol. LXV (Spring, 1966), 190; John A. Garraty, "The Nature of Biography," in Eisenstadt, *The Craft of American History*, II, 58; Tholfsen, *Historical Thinking: An Introduction*, 322.

Even the most superficial examination of historical causation quickly reveals the inability of historians to arrive at any single formula or method which explains satisfactorily the character of the causative process. Whether the investigation is aimed at the larger issues in historiography—the fall of Rome, the origins of the French Revolution, the causes of the Reformation or of the American Civil War, or the assessment of guilt for World War I—or whether it is focused upon lesser episodes—the failure of Lee at Gettysburg, Napoleon's decision to return from Elba, Martin Luther's inner motivation, or an explanation of the social setting which produced the phenomenon of McCarthyism—the result is inevitably the same. Different historians arrive at varying conclusions. Moreover, these conclusions often possess equal validity, being supported by evidence sometimes gathered from the same sources and striking the reader as offering valuable insights into the nature of the problem under consideration. In fact, one of the most popular publishing devices of recent times has been to prepare books of historical essays which provide the reader with examples of conflicting interpretations, usually grouped under what are deemed provocative titles such as "conflict or consensus?" "evolution or revolution?" and other appellations designed to ensnare the interest of the undergraduate.

One explanation for the multiple character of causal hypotheses has traditionally been to attribute such pluralism to the subjective operation of the historian himself. This familiar relativist argument has much to recommend it, although in its own way it too assumes the reality, however unattainable, of *the* cause lurking unseen behind the screens of historical subjectivity. What is more convincing and likely is the reality of multiple causation. Both our personal life experiences and our contacts with the world of nature would seem to confirm that opinion. Our own decisions are the result of many operating factors, some unconscious and some conscious, and we are quick to acknowledge the fact. All natural processes are also the result of many contributing forces. No informed person would attempt to argue, for instance, that the creation of a fusion bomb or

Other relevant comments are to be found in William O. Aydelotte, "Quantification in History," *American Historical Review*, Vol. LXXI (April, 1966), 804.

the operation of the kidney or the pollination of plants could be explained by a single and inflexible formula. Why, then, should the study of history be any different? Since history concerns itself with the most difficult of all explanations, causation in human affairs, it would be unrealistic to expect anything but what indeed we do get—multiple explanations.

Historians have also been cautioned to remember that preoccupation with the complexities and convolutions of causation should not blind them to the fact that causation is but one historiographical problem. Being able to determine cause in any logical rationale of thought which proves acceptable to fellow historians or even to the general public does not mean that the totality of history has been explored. The historian is more than an explainer; as Cushing Strout has commented, "Whatever some philosophers may say, he [the historian] knows that explanation is broader than causal explication."[6] Description, analysis, biography, and narrative are also of some importance. Excessive concentration upon the inner dynamics of the whys of history may lead the historian down the garden path of logical regularity, away from the chaos and illogic which so frequently appear to be the main components of historical reality. The desire to see pattern and system where none exists is a common affliction of mankind, and certainly historians are not immune from its blandishments. While there may usually exist an intimacy and causal relationship between events as they succeed one another, it does not necessarily follow that they always possess a cause-and-effect correlation. The result of such myopia can often be a deterioration of causality into little more than the detection of the regularity of sequence.[7]

Likewise, the temptation to place historical events into a kind of lockstep easily leads to what Isaiah Berlin has termed the sin of historical inevitability. The historian, properly, has to be more concerned with what did happen rather than with what did not

[6] Strout, "Causation and the American Civil War: Two Appraisals," *History and Theory*, Vol. I, No. II (1961), 182.

[7] This tendency is thoroughly examined in a perceptive article by Thomas N. Bonner, "Civil War Historians and the Needless War," *Journal of the History of Ideas*, Vol. XVII (April, 1956). See especially p. 193.

occur. But, in dealing only with what he believes to be historical reality, he may forget that options, alternative courses, were available to historical actors in any given situation of the past. Theodore Roosevelt could have refused to run for the third term in 1912; Germany might have rejected the Austrian plea for support against Serbia in July, 1914; Luther could have submitted to papal authority at the Diet of Worms. Practically any historical event or decision could be offered in evidence to buttress a cautious and tentative view of historical causation. Yet the dilemma remains, and historians often find themselves in a logical quandary: the historian must explain what in fact did occur and at the same time be aware of the many turnings in the road that were ignored. Acutely aware of both the tragic nature of man and his history, the thoughtful historian has had to confess that the roots of causality are often hidden from his sight.[8]

When those who are not professional historians demand that the writer of history offer a scheme of explanation which will guide mankind in much the same manner that the observations of the chemist can warn of the peril inherent in the admixture of certain compounds, they are not only asking the impossible but also missing one of the principal characteristics of the nature of history: its particularity. The historian has learned to be wary of the universal axiom, the all-embracing pattern, and justifiably so. For what the historian has learned through painstaking research is that each historical event has a certain integrity of its own and does not lend itself easily to either past or future linkage. And this truism applies as much to causation as to any other aspect of historical investigation. "When an historian seeks to explain a particular action," commented Leonard Krieger, "what he wants explained is precisely the particularity of the action; why it was produced by this man at this place at this time."[9]

In addition to the particularity of each historical situation the

[8] Howard K. Beale has written candidly of this problem in *Theodore Roosevelt and the Rise of America to World Power*, 5. See also the comments of Don E. Fehrenbacher, "Comment on Why the Republican Party Came to Power," in George H. Knoles (ed.), *The Crisis of the Union, 1860–1861*, 23–24.

[9] Leonard Krieger, "Comments on Historical Explanation," in Sidney Hook (ed.), *Philosophy and History: A Symposium*, 137.

historian has to consider the uniqueness of individuals and the backgrounds of their motivations if he is to examine all of the strands entwined in the rope of causation.[10] One does not have to endorse completely the claim of Sidney Mead that "the ascertainment of motives is the chief goal of historical studies,"[11] to agree to the importance of the individual and his desires and aims as a major guiding force in the determination of history. And individual motivation, which is difficult enough for the psychologist trained in the analysis of human behavior, is doubly difficult for the historian, who must perform a precarious balancing act when dealing with individual people and their reasons for acting as they do. "Historians cannot emphasize universals because history must include change. They cannot center only on individuals because they must accept the responsibility for explanation."[12]

The tension between the rational and the irrational, between the traditional and the new, between the particularity and the totality of the historical experience, and between the desire for simplicity and the reality of multiplicity are all nearly imponderable for the historian in his attempts to uncover the sources of causality in history. Traditionally, however, the two problems which have occupied most of his attention have been those of deciding how much of history can be explained in terms of those events which preceded the event under consideration and how much can be explained in terms of contingency and chance. The simple solution suggested by H. Stuart Hughes, namely, that "the most satisfactory type of causal explanation in history simply tries to locate the factor which, when removed, would make the decisive difference in a given sequence of events,"[13] has not been generally accepted by the historians of the postwar period. Rather, since 1945 historians in

[10] This subject has already been discussed in some detail in Chapter 4, but the question of individual motivation has a fundamental bearing on causation as well.

[11] Mead, "Church History Explained," *Church History*, Vol. XXXII (March, 1963), 20.

[12] E. N. Peterson, "Historical Scholarship and World Unity," *Social Research*, Vol. XXVII (January, 1961), 443.

[13] Hughes, "The Historian and the Social Scientist," *American Historical Review*, Vol. LXVI (October, 1960), 29.

America have once again argued the merits of continuity and contingency as basic determinants in the process of causation. Not too surprisingly, the result of this renewed investigation has been not a single answer but several answers. Ironically, the admission that history itself is plural in essence has had to be extended to historical studies of causation as well. Advocates of continuity and the champions of contingency have advanced valuable insights into the causal process.

The vogue of scientific history which pervaded American historical thought in the half century between 1875 and 1925 left as one of its legacies to the historical profession a fundamental faith in the efficacy of historical development as an efficient and comprehensive device for understanding not only the past but also the present. Institutions, revolutions, wars, social habit and custom, even the lives of individuals, it was thought, could be interpreted and explained only in the light of their history. Gathering much of its inspiration from the German historicist school, scientific historians in America began to emphasize the continuity of history at the expense of the different and the new. Many went so far as to claim that particularity and the seemingly endless configurations of historical events were illusory. The enduring qualities of the study of history were the similarities and seeds of the future that were encountered at every turn. It was simple, therefore, to equate causality with continuity, to seek to unravel the encrusted complexity of any historical episode by unraveling the accretions of the past. This theory, carried to its logical extremity, argued that the past, however remote, might well contain those elements which contributed, at any given moment in time, to an historical fact. And it did not matter whether that "fact" happened to be a war, a constitution, or an idea.

The habit of viewing events within a historical context was substantially reinforced by the impact of evolutionary thought which was making such revolutionary waves in the intellectual milieu at about the same time. For, if Darwinism meant anything at all, it meant that life forms were to be understood as the end result of a developmental process governed by the law of natural selection. Even those historians who, like Henry Adams, rejected the ultimate implication of progress in Darwinism were profoundly influenced by evolutionary ideas. There was, consequently, a marriage in historical writing between the complementary ideas of continuity and evolutionary growth, a wedding which numbered among its offspring both works of brilliant insight and those of strait-jacketed narrowness. On the one hand, encouragement was given to detect many hitherto unrelated and unexplained phenomena of the past, and on the other hand, disdain was shown for the flash of creative intuition as a legitimate method of historical investigation. Even the relativist assault against the framework of scientific history in the 1920's and 1930's failed to dislodge completely the almost automatic assumption that continuity was the primary ingredient of history and the best guide to determining causation.[14]

The cadre of American historians who had come to professional maturity during the first thirty years of the century carried with them into the postwar era a general confidence in the empirical reality of historical continuity. A statement by one of the deans of the profession reflected this faith in its most undiluted form. Writing in 1959, J. Franklin Jameson declared:

At the basis of our confidence lies the belief, which the last half-century's studies have converted into settled doctrine, that the whole civilization of the present has its roots deep in the past, and can never be understood except by entering deeply into the study of origins. The stream of history is a stream of causation. The spacious fabric that lies before us, woven for us on the roaring loom of time, gray and dull in some lights or aspects, shot with gleams of splendor when seen in others, is composed of threads drawn from every age of the past.[15]

[14] Alexander Gerschenkron has identified five elements as comprising the historian's concept of continuity: (1) constancy of direction—for example, the spread of democratic government to 1914, (2) periodicity of events—the periodic re-creation of similar situations, (3) endogenous change—one that is described in terms of a homogeneous set of factors, (4) length of causal regress—the singling out of the beginning of a causal chain, and (5) stability of the rate of change—for example, price movements. See his "On the Concept of Continuity in History," American Philosophical Association *Proceedings*, Vol. CVI (June 29, 1962), 200–206.

[15] Jameson, "The Future Uses of History," *American Historical Review*, Vol. LXV (October, 1959), 64.

The distinguished Carlton J. H. Hayes urged fellow members of the American Historical Association not to "lose sight of the continuity of history." Arguing against a cataclysmic or apocalyptic view of history, Hayes maintained that events which often appear to be inexplicably abrupt were not really cataclysmic at all but "merely speeded some continuous process long previously under way and left untouched vastly more habits of human thought and action than they altered." Robert S. Cotterill in a presidential address to the Southern Historical Association characterized the student of history as one who "is insistent on sequence and consequence" and who "demands continuity and cause." Cotterill insisted that "every historical event" considered by the historian "must have a family tree as an accessory before the fact."[16]

The latter part of Cotterill's statement contains the significant element of commonality which all such declarations hold to be the essential feature of historical causation, namely, the unbroken line of continuity which preceded the event. Within such a framework the historian can operate solely in the area he knows best—the past. Moreover, it is a predictable past, one which possesses variables to be sure, but one, nevertheless, which can be reduced to a set of observable factors if only the historian has the requisite powers of detection. Under these circumstances the web of history may be indeed a tangled skein, but it is a skein which can be unraveled if the historian has the patience and the skill. He need not fret about the introduction of any new threads. After untying the knot, he has only to follow the various threads backward to understand the sources of causation.

This approach has much to recommend it, for, undeniably, the past is the route to the present, and certainly a primary function of the historian is a close examination of the historical past. Yet if the

---

16 Hayes, "The American Frontier—Frontier of What?" *American Historical Review,* Vol. LI (January, 1946), 214–15; Robert S. Cotterill, "The Old South to the New," *Journal of Southern History,* Vol. XV (February, 1949), 5. See also the statements by Leo Gershoy, "Carl Becker on Progress and Power," *American Historical Review,* Vol. LV (October, 1949), 22; and Donald C. Swift and Rodney Allen, "History Instruction and Human Aspirations: A Proposed Synthesis," *Social Studies,* Vol. LVII (January, 1966), 4.

historian spends all of his time in an examination of those developmental strands which have led to a certain event, he runs the risk of not looking closely enough at the event itself. Correlative to this danger is the tendency for the historian with this frame of reference to speak more frequently of "underlying" or "fundamental" causes. He persistently makes the distinction between these underlying factors and what he usually terms "immediate" causes. The implication becomes clear when stated within such a context: immediate causes are never quite as important as those more deeply embedded in the past. Consequently, the tendency to ignore the actual event under consideration is further enhanced. By examining two instances, one involving a major and pivotal event in modern history—the French Revolution—and the other a more limited occurrence—the Anglo-American debate over military strategy during World War II—it will be possible to see how a faith in continuity can shape the mold of historical perception.

Perhaps no event since the Reformation of the sixteenth century has so occupied the attention of historians as has the revolutionary fever which began in France in 1789 and soon engulfed not only Europe but other continents as well. Most students of the Revolution have agreed about its far-reaching effects for the growth of liberalism and democracy and its influence on the origins of modern totalitarianism. That the Revolution was a cataclysmic event of almost indescribable proportions remains undisputed, and, because this fact has been universally recognized, historians have naturally desired to penetrate the façade of violence and change, to delineate and understand those deep-rooted forces which were climaxed by the storming of the Bastille and the Tennis Court Oath.

In the nearly two centuries which now have passed since the days of Robespierre and Bonaparte, practically all avenues of historical causation have been explored. Those writers, Marxist and otherwise, who perceive economic factors as primary have described the clash of economic interests between a growing middle class and an inherently feudal and increasingly anachronistic aristocracy. They have likewise pointed to the long-standing dissatisfaction of the agricultural peasantry with absentee ownership of land, inequitable and unrealistic taxation, and the absence of a satisfactory currency. The significance of a burgeoning industrialism and the subsequent creation of an urban proletariat has not been ignored, nor has the profound role played in the economic system by the Church escaped scrutiny. Those who have sought comprehension within the more traditional framework of political activity have discovered many factors and forces which help explain the revolutionary upheaval. Among causes for unrest and dissatisfaction noted have been the conflicting and unwieldy sets of laws which accompanied the maze of jurisdictional agencies, the tradition of French absolutism and its historic unwillingness to share its power, the caprice of king and nobility which so often resulted in chronic debt and financial mismanagement, and the conduct of a foreign policy frequently unrealistic in its aspirations and too demanding of dwindling French resources.

Intellectual historians have also had much to say about the origins of the Revolution. Their examinations of the chief currents in European thought in the seventeenth and eighteenth centuries have emphasized the growth of rationalism under the benevolent spirit of the Enlightenment. The writings of the famous French *philosophes*, Voltaire, Rousseau, and Montesquieu, it has been suggested, were in reality incendiaries which contributed materially to the eventual overthrow of the monarchy and the final dissolution of the *ancien régime*. All these "causes" are but a small number of those which have been discussed by historians eager to reveal the fundamental determinants of the Revolution. No one would argue that their researches have not been valuable and illuminating, but it is impossible to assert with finality that any or all the causal factors adequately explain why the turmoil occurred in that fateful year of 1789. Nor do these explanations, in and by themselves, account for the new, explosive situations which occurred after the opening of the Revolution (the use of the *levée en masse* comes quickly to mind). We are left then with the conclusion that the causal factors in any given historical situation, especially one of the magnitude of the French Revolution, can never completely explain the event. This seems to be true in both a quantitative and a qualitative sense. Causation, especially that which attempts to explain those momentous events which result in great change, is obviously more complicated than the coming together of the threads of continuity. Continuity would seem to be only a partial explanation, not the entire answer.

Similar observations are encountered when one descends from the contemplation of major historical problems to a consideration of those of a lesser import. A case in point is the manner in which historians of World War II have explained the different approaches to military strategy advocated by the British and the Americans between 1942 and 1944. What was in contention was the best method of ensuring Germany's defeat. There was no disagreement that this objective should constitute the primary Allied consideration; that had been formally decided at the ARCADIA conference held in Washington in late December, 1941, and early January, 1942. The British, led by the persuasive rhetoric of Winston Churchill, argued for a "closing the ring" strategy: intensified naval blockade, a bomber offensive against the industrial centers of the Reich, the securing of the sea lanes, especially in the Mediterranean, aid to resistance groups on the Continent, peripheral attacks against exposed and vulnerable German outposts, such as those in North Africa, and, finally, executed as a finishing stroke, a cross-channel invasion. The Americans insisted, on the other hand, that the cross-channel thrust be given top priority and that all other considerations were secondary, since they would divert and weaken the effort to invade France and strike at the heart of Germany.

Historians attempting to explain the divergence of views have generally alluded to the historical experience of each nation as the essential factor in their respective attitudes toward the problem of military strategy. The British, it is argued, throughout their history have never possessed either the manpower or the resources to confront a major enemy in a direct confrontation on land without first having weakened their adversary in a series of steps similar to those urged by Churchill in 1942. England's experience, first adumbrated in the long struggle with France for continental supremacy which culminated so disastrously for her in 1453, had made her wary of committing herself to European engagements in which the logistic advantages rested entirely with the enemy. Moreover, this piece of conventional wisdom had seemingly been confirmed by the successes which the British had enjoyed in the wars against the hegemonies of the Hapsburgs and the Bourbons and especially in the titanic fight against Napoleon in the dark days between 1800 and 1815. With this background most historians have felt that the World War I experience proved decisive in shaping British policy in 1942. The memories of the tragedy of the trenches, of the enormous losses incurred on the Somme, and the subsequent enfeebling of the empire were still too fresh for the advocacy of any policy which might recapitulate the situation. Long-standing tradition then, reinforced by Churchill's own obsession with the possibilities of Mediterranean campaigns, were the principal components of the British opposition to the American desire to engage the forces of Hitler as quickly and as directly as possible. This explanation for British motivation emphasizes heavily the forces of continuity and interprets English intransigence as a logical development of English history.

Similarly, the American advocacy of a massive assault across the English Channel has been viewed as the result of the particular experiences of the United States, which were largely determined by the spacious nature of the American environment, an abundance of manpower, and an equally abundant supply of the sinews of war. Most frequently cited as examples of the American predilection for direct military action were the drive from Veracruz to Mexico City during the Mexican War, the Union tactics employed against the Confederacy, especially as formed by Ulysses S. Grant in the last year of the Civil War, the invasion of Cuba in 1898, and the American drive on the Meuse-Argonne front in the spring of 1918. The appeal of General Grant's famous statement about fighting it out on the line if it took all summer was undeniable. Americans, historians contended, also interpreted the World War I situation from an entirely different perspective from that of their English allies. Germany was defeated in the first encounter, Americans believed, only when American manpower and firepower made the difference between the opposing forces so overwhelming as to be irresistible. Just as the threads of historical continuity dictated the British position, so the same historical record shaped American arguments. According to these hypotheses, the "present" of 1942 could be satisfactorily explained in terms of historical continuity which often had its roots very deep in the past. In a very real sense continuity itself became a causal explanation.

But nagging doubts linger. Can continuity explain causation with any greater precision for the microcosm than it can for the macrocosm? While it is undeniably true that a close examination of events in sequence can give much illumination to an understanding of a given historical situation, such an investigation does not tell us why a particular thing happened at the exact moment in time that it did. The French Revolution could have occurred at many points both before and after 1789; but it did not. Therefore, it would seem reasonable to assume that something unique and special occurred in that year to produce the conflagration which ensued. Likewise, was there something about the "present" situation in 1942 which helped to determine the variant attitudes of England and the United States toward the proper military strategy to be used against Germany? Continuity has come, therefore, to be seen by many historians as only a partial explanation, and the faith of the scientific historian in a rather rigid historicism has been seriously questioned in the postwar years.

The most important single obstacle to the development of a theory which posits continuity as the major element in causation is the problem of accounting for change in history. Like so many other areas investigated and discussed by historians after 1945, the mechanics of change, of altered direction in the flow of history, was something which historians had always been forced to concern themselves about; it was by no means a novel philosophical and methodological problem. But there was a fresh urgency connected with its re-examination, and the habit of explaining the present solely in terms of the paths leading to the present appeared to be inadequate. As Cushing Strout observed: "If the historian were to deduce consequences from antecedents, there would be nothing in the former, not found in the latter. How then could he speak of anything new happening at all?"[17]

The simplest solution would have been to ignore the problem, to define history in its narrowest terms, and to interpret the task of the historian only in its narrative function. Such an approach, however, would not only have been a refusal to face the issue squarely, but it would also have been self-defeating, for there is certainly no guarantee that one would not have to wrestle with the intangibles of change in a strictly narrative historical account. Furthermore, much of the best written history has occurred because historians after times of great upheaval and change within their societies have tried to understand what had happened by seeking comprehension through a study of history.[18] Change simply cannot be avoided, nor can the historian escape dealing with its inner dynamic or the challenge it offers to the notion of continuity.

Some historians have attempted to solve the problem, at least semantically, by making change in the larger sense a part of continuity. Richard Van Alstyne has declared that "ceaseless change is the law of history," and Arthur Bestor believes that "the unique concern of history" has been with change, "not change affecting one particularized area of human affairs."[19] But merely recognizing the existence of change or even elevating it to the status of law does not instruct the working historian how to deal effectively with it in the area of causation. Nor does it answer the question of how does change fit into a pattern of continuity. Can change and continuity really be reconciled? Does not the existence of one challenge the validity of the other, especially if one is attempting to determine a major causative agent? The matter is further complicated when an effort is made to define more accurately what change means spe-

[17] Strout, "Causation and the American Civil War," *History and Theory*, Vol. I, No. II (1961), 177.

[18] Felix Gilbert, review of Gerhard Ritter, *Geschicte Als Bildungsmacht* in *American Historical Review*, Vol. LIII (July, 1948), 787. Gilbert offers Thucydides, Guicciardini, Clarendon, Ranke, and Tocqueville as examples.

[19] Richard W. Van Alstyne, "History and the Imagination," *Pacific Historical Review*, Vol. XXXIII (February, 1964), 19; Bestor, "The Humaneness of History," in Eisenstadt (ed.), *The Craft of American History*, I, 12.

cifically to historians. For the student who is trying to describe a particular historical phenomenon, whether it be the reasons for Solon's decrees or the wars of Charles XII of Sweden or the election of Rutherford B. Hayes to the American presidency, generalizations about generic change have little practical value. "The historian is not primarily concerned with change as an ongoing process, or with formulating laws that may govern that process; his concern is with one particular phase of change, with one grouping of events that is by definition unique."[20] Similarly, the historian whose main concern is the continuity of events runs the risk of losing the sense of "the connections of each particular event with its antecedents and consequences."[21] The only sensible deduction to be made is that neither change nor continuity can survive without the other; they are both integral parts of history. Preoccupation with one or the other produces distortion and ignores the immanence of both. Crane Brinton put it best: "Yet what endures is surely at least as 'real' as what changes."[22]

The reaction against an unquestioning faith in the ability of the forces of continuity to explain the historical process produced a renewal of interest in the role played by contingency or chance in the drama of human history. The accidental, the unique, the unexpected had always exercised a fascination for the human imagination and had long been a favorite theme of religion, poetry, and philosophy; the tragic notion that doomed man is at the mercy of a capricious universe has bemused the contemplative from the time of Sophocles to the days of the "Whiffenpoof Song." Historiography also contains similar examples. Roman historians spoke frequently of *fortuna*, or "chance," as the one element that could not be anticipated when recounting the affairs of man. The Middle Ages with their emphasis upon history as the unfolding of a providential plan found little room

20 Willcox, "An Historian Looks at Social Change," in Eisenstadt (ed.), *The Craft of American History*, I, 23. The converse also applied: history cannot be understood only by its uniqueness. This point is made by Trygve Tholfsen in his discussion of Thucydides. See Tholfsen, *Historical Thinking: An Introduction*, 19.

21 Hexter, *Reappraisals in History*, 22.

22 Brinton, "Many Mansions," *American Historical Review*, Vol. LXIX (January, 1964), 311.

for the accidental and the capricious, preferring to ascribe to the inexplicable and the unexpected the inscrutable motives of the deity, whose designs were often hidden from an ignorant and sinful mankind. However, with the renewal of interest in classical civilization which characterized the Renaissance, historians once again discovered the significance of fortuitousness in history.

Both Niccolò Machiavelli and Francesco Guicciardini found chance a significant element in the history of the Italian peninsula. And in *The Prince* the former advised neophyte statesmen to be alert to the possibilities for advancement which might from time to time present themselves unexpectedly. Historians of the Enlightenment, especially Edward Gibbon, Voltaire, and David Hume, with their heavy emphasis upon the human capacity for rational thought, once again preferred to explain the past in terms that left little room for the play of accidental events. Engaged in a monumental undertaking to elevate the study of history to a discipline founded on the principles of Cartesian logic, the historians of the eighteenth century eschewed approaches which seemed to exalt the irrational or the unforeseen. This trend was reinforced by the development of the "scientific" school of German scholarship in the mid-nineteenth century. Particularly important was the attitude of confidence and certainty which accompanied the monographic production of historians committed to a faith in the knowability of the past. Major intellectual currents of the century further served to buttress this surety; Darwinism, Marxism, and Hegelianism certainly had in common the assumption that a historical process undergird development and that this development traveled along a predetermined route, whether that highway was charted by natural selection, the class struggle, or the world spirit. Such mechanism had no place in its dynamic for contingency. What might appear to the uninitiated observer to be the happenstance of fate was in reality the result of forces, which, if properly understood, were quite predictable. Consequently, that meticulous historian J. B. Bury could announce to those who heard his first lecture at Cambridge University in 1902 that "history was a science, no more and no less."[23]

23 J. B. Bury, *Selected Essays* (ed. by H. Temperley), 3–22.

In 1916, Bury was no longer as sure as he once had been. In an article which deserves wider readership, entitled "Cleopatra's Nose," Bury revealed that his experience as a historian had convinced him that the fact of contingency, of chance occurrence, had to be considered by the historian as a factor in understanding causation.[24] Twentieth-century experience was crucial in undermining the previously held faith; modern physics and mathematics spoke of relativity and the principle of indeterminancy; Freud and other investigators of the unconscious revealed the existence of the irrational and often hidden depths of human motivation. But the very fact of enormous change in technology and industry, the growth of totalitarian schemes, and the omnipresence of mass slaughter were the obvious subversives. Once again historians considered the matter of contingency as an agent within the causal process, and, as was the case with continuity, they reached an ambivalent conclusion.

The key to any honest evaluation of contingency and its significance obviously lay in its relationship to change in history. As has been hitherto observed, it was in change that continuity lost itself. Could it be, some asked, that contingency might explain that elusive process where continuity had failed? Roy F. Nichols noted that historians were free to experiment with new concepts, that precision of statement often did not fit the pattern of "haphazard confusion in human behavior" that it attempted to duplicate, and that the availability of alternative options in any given situation was frequently overlooked. Furthermore, Nichols declared that "there are much less determinism and a higher frequency of accident in the processes of change." Writing from the viewpoint of the economic historian, Abbott P. Usher also commented on the enigma of change. "There are discontinuities that invite change," said Usher. "The essential feature of history is the emergence of novelty." Yet mere recognition of chance as a factor in the mechanics of change did not solve the problem of either explaining or anticipating its operation. To some, like Folke Dovring, the extent to which events were the result of hazard made them both inexplicable and useless.[25] The pessimism

24 *Ibid.*, 60–69.
25 Nichols, "History in a Self-governing Culture," *American Historical Review*,

implicit in the latter proposition rested, however, upon a rather limited view of the function of the historian and even further on a restrictive interpretation of the nature of history. What Dovring stated was true in the limited view that history was concerned generally with the universal event and its reappearance throughout history. When the role of the individual and the results of his actions were taken into account, the matter of contingency acquired more meaning.

Historians have almost automatically and nearly unanimously associated the operation of chance happenings in history with either the deliberate or the unintentional activities of individual human beings. Even the deliberate act of a human agent may carry with it unanticipated consequences.[26] From the shape of Cleopatra's nose to the assassination of a prince or president the definition of the chance event has most often been conceived as the end result of a series of events which have been triggered by the actions or activities of an individual human agent. One of the reasons for the charm of the contingency approach to the problem of historical causation has been its implicit endorsement that the individual does in fact count for something. If one transplants the ancient philosophical dualism of free will versus predestination, contingency champions the former view in history, and continuity identifies with the latter. The analogy is not all that distinct, but there is something of the same flavor to the arguments advanced by historians as that which accompanied the earlier philosophical and theological debates. Certainly a study of history which recognizes the possibility of chance affecting the movement of history at the same time admits the potentiality of individual human direction. Conversely, while men may initiate through some action of their own the chance event, other men often become the victims or objects of that identical event. Edward Channing was conscious of this paradox in his great work, and

Vol. LXXII (January, 1967), 421; Abbot P. Usher, "The Significance of Modern Empiricism for History and Economics," *Journal of Economic History*, Vol. IX (November, 1949), 149; Dovring, *History as a Social Science*, 54.

26 A good discussion of this aspect of contingency may be found in Tholfsen, *Historical Thinking: An Introduction*, 283.

historians of the more recent period have also been quick to note this facet of evaluating the role of chance in history. Yet it remains a somewhat obvious truism that the appearance of the unexpected happening prevents any historian from making accurate forecasts about the future, and the primary reason for his predictive inability, Louis Gottschalk said, was "because of the variability of human behavior."[27]

The postwar trend has been, therefore, for historians in America to concede that contingency is a part of the causal formula without dismissing the significance of continuity or allowing the association of chance with individual action to deteriorate into a "great man" theory of history. W. B. Willcox warned his professional colleagues that the working historian must not only determine the impersonal forces involved in causation but also "weigh the effect of sheer accident." Arthur Schlesinger, Jr., declared that the historian must be ever alert to his natural desire to "tidy up the past." He believed that the student of contemporary history, faced with the reality of the speed and bewilderment of current events will "know better and give adequate scope to the play of contingency, chance, ignorance, and sheer stupidity." William H. McNeill put the matter most succinctly: "History is indeed full of surprises and accidents, some of them trivial in their consequences, others of profound importance."[28]

[27] John De Novo, "Edward Channing's 'Great Work' Twenty Years After," *Mississippi Valley Historical Review*, Vol. XXXIX (September, 1952), 261–62; Louis Gottschalk, "Causes of Revolution," *American Journal of Sociology*, Vol. L (July, 1944), 3.

[28] Willcox, "An Historian Looks at Social Change," in Eisenstadt (ed.), *The Craft of American History*, I, 20; Arthur M. Schlesinger, Jr., "On the Writing of Contemporary History," *Atlantic*, Vol. CC (March, 1967), 74; William H. McNeill, *Past and Future*, 1. In a delightful autobiography Bernadotte Schmitt related his encounters with historical contingency: "The best illustration I know of is the murder at Sarajevo in June 1914, which set off the First World War. After the first attempt to kill the Archduke Francis Ferdinand had failed, the plans of the royal party were somewhat changed, but the chauffeur of his car was not told of the new route and at a certain corner he began to turn, as originally prescribed. He was forced to stop and back up—and at that moment the assassin Princip, standing there, seized his chance to shoot. But for this mishap, it is unlikely that the Archduke would have been killed and therefore most improbable that war would have

Mere recognition of the presence of contingency in history did not solve the problem of historical causation or make the historian's task any simpler; indeed, this awareness was an enormously complicating factor. But the historian, in facing the fact that historical causation was complicated, was on the path to the kind of wisdom which a complicated society demanded. If the experience was often frustrating, it was also humbling, a humiliation which was prerequisite to a deeper understanding. The historian had come a long way toward that goal when he understood that "history's only iron law was irony."[29] Causality was involved in both continuity and contingency; neither was the only key to the locked door of the why of history. It is a major advancement that historians since World War II have accepted the pluralism inherent in historical causation.

broken out in the summer of 1914. At Gallipoli, in 1915, the Turks had exhausted their ammunition after the great attack of March 18 and were preparing to flee as soon as the Allies renewed their attack the next day—which they did not do. In our day, we remember that the Japanese were not detected approaching Pearl Harbor because the officer responsible for searching the skies had gone off duty and had not been replaced. In an earlier time, neither Lee nor Meade had planned to fight at Gettysburg, but met there by accident. The role of chance, *fortuna* the Romans called it, must not be exaggerated, but is sometimes just as important as great forces and the actions of great men." *The Fashion and Future of History*, 8.

[29] Herbert Feis, "The Prankishness of History," *Virginia Quarterly Review*, Vol. XL (Winter, 1956), 58–66.

The more the historian is led to reflect upon the problems of causality within the historical process the more does he confront the dilemma of whether or not history can afford answers to the larger philosophical questions of human existence. Does history present to its students any intimation of discernible pattern which offers solution to that most ancient of queries, Whither mankind? Most historians since 1945 have been willing to grant that the extraction of generalizations from their studies has been a legitimate function of their craft,[1] but there has been less enthusiasm for engaging in the kind of sweeping synthesis suggested by Toynbee in his famous *Study of History.* Naturally, historians have been reluctant to step over the boundary between history and philosophy of history into that area that may be conveniently termed metahistory. Not only have the canons of scientific historiography acted as a deterrent but also the memory of how history had been manipulated by Hegel, Marx, and myriad other system builders has remained fresh enough to make writers of history exceedingly wary of those who would substitute history for religion or philosophy. Yet, despite the caution of most historians, significant and growing numbers have been willing to admit the validity of metahistory as a proper subject for professional attention. Indeed, in light of the popular acclaim given Toynbee's massive history and the wide distribution of its abridgment, historians in America, as well as those abroad, were compelled once again to make metahistory a viable subject for appraisal and debate.

There can be little doubt that it was Toynbee's *Study of History*

---

1 See the discussion of this point in Chapter 4.

which rekindled the arguments concerning the appropriate place of metahistory in the world of the professional historian. A two-volume abridgment by D. C. Somervell was a Book-of-the-Month Club selection in 1947, and historians in America were drawn to the conclusion that Toynbee had answered a deeply felt need, that he had made the sweep of history seem immediate and significant to a large number of people. That, by itself, was insufficient pressure to cause consternation within guild ranks; H. G. Wells, who had enjoyed similar public acclaim two decades earlier, had been dismissed by most historians as an imaginative but amateurish popularizer whose history was on the same level with his science fiction. But Toynbee could not be ignored so easily; he was no amateur. He had all the requisite scholarly credentials; he was a profoundly learned man whose wide-ranging erudition impressed even those who found fault with his synthetic generalizations. Indeed, this was precisely the point: because Toynbee's membership rights in the lists of the academic professionals were unquestionable, he had to be taken seriously. That he had breached the accepted canons of historiography to go beyond the mundane to the matter of ultimate meaning was something that could be neither overlooked nor dealt with summarily. Toynbee did not represent an attack from the outside, but rather he seemed to many to personify the insidious forces of apostasy—a threat to the existing structure of historiography. Yet he was not without allies within the historical community in America, and they viewed Toynbee and his work as necessary agents in the attempt to make the historian a more meaningful figure in the postatomic world.

Toynbee's challenge to the existing pattern of historical writing consisted roughly of a three-part assault: in addition to the detection of patterns in history which implied the suprahistorical, he also reasserted the validity of universal history and the use of the comparative method in historical analysis. There was nothing new or original in any of the three; indeed it was the fact that most historians considered them outworn and discredited that contributed to much of the antagonism with which the *Study of History* was greeted. The long struggle toward a history free of predetermined hypotheses and imposed theological interpretation had been littered with the debris of similar constructs. There was a natural reluctance to readmit into the historiographical mainstream anything which might threaten the freedom and independence of historical writing—a freedom which had taken so very long to win. Yet a certain paradox almost immediately presented itself: Did not this highly prized liberty apply equally to Toynbee and his followers? Did not the free market place of ideas, so valued by historians, have a stall where Toynbeean concepts might be examined without a sign declaring that they were old and damaged goods? The ambivalence thus produced was responsible for much of the tension and emotion which characterized the discussion of Toynbee's ideas.

Universal history has been most closely associated in Western historical thought with the emergence of Christian historiography during the fourth and fifth centuries after Christ. Augustine and his co-worker Orosius, in attempting to counteract the pagan claim that Christianity was largely to blame for the Roman time of troubles, were forced to argue from a perspective larger than their own point in time. And Augustine also took the opportunity to posit a philosophy of history which examined the whole of human history for its *rationale* rather than limiting itself to the history of a single people or political unit. Since Christ had become a savior for Gentile as well as Jew, it was necessary to use the entire scope of history as a backdrop. All history, therefore, Augustine asserted, must begin with Adam and progress in linear fashion to the present time. History could then demonstrate in many and often surprising ways the unfolding of God's providence and saving grace in the affairs of all men in all times. While this stricture did much to eliminate the provincialism and snobbery often found in Roman historiography, it paradoxically imposed a narrower base of interpretation and meaning, for it limited the questions which the historian could ask of his material. In a way it was as if a forest, hitherto hidden to the eye, suddenly came into view, but the viewer was forbidden to examine anything but the oak trees he encountered there. Universal history, then, was Christian history and became connected in Western thought with the unfolding of Christian apologetics.

Medieval historians followed the Augustinian tradition, although more often in theory than in practice. It is true, of course, that writers of history in the Middle Ages seldom went beyond the chronicle, but in theory at least they adhered to the belief that universal history was the proper setting for written history. The rupture with Christian historiography, most clearly demonstrated in the eighteenth-century Enlightenment, did not, however, also break with the tradition of universal history. Voltaire is remembered, among other things, for advocating the writing of the history of all nations. What the writers of the Enlightenment did was to secularize the approach. To carry out the above metaphor, they encouraged historians to look at maple and sycamore trees in addition to the oaks. Yet, if it is true that Christian observers were constantly on the alert for signs of heavenly intervention, it is equally true that the rationalists relied heavily on a concept which bespoke another determinant—the idea of progress. The school of scientific historiography, developing in the mid-nineteenth century, then, viewed universal history as being intimately related with either a religious or a secular faith, and, although the revered founder of the scientific school Leopold von Ranke urged his disciples to undertake the study of universal history in a scientific spirit, the prevailing temper was to forgo universal history for more manageable units of study.

Toynbee's employment of the comparative method likewise aroused opposition. That opposition was the more intense because of the mammoth horizons encompassed by the scope of his efforts. Specialists were quick to object to his intellectual pretensions and to the idea that a solitary scholar could command enough information about the entirety of human history to formulate valid syntheses about anything as complex as the rise and fall of civilizations. Toynbee's far-ranging analogies, his willingness to see comparisons and contrasts between societies removed from each other in both space and time, and his seeming arbitrariness in the selection and evaluation of disparate data were all subjects for the criticism of his colleagues. Additionally, like the matter of universal history to which it was closely related, the comparative method was tarnished with the stain of having been the companion of discredited philosophies and interpretations of history. For many historians this guilt by association was sufficient for rejection. It was much too easy, many insisted, to discover in history whatever one desired to find; superficial similarities abounded in the vast amounts of information which had been collected concerning the histories of civilizations, and it was impossible for one man to gain sufficient mastery over these materials to make any kind of meaningful comparative study. Furthermore, as Toynbee's work came more and more to reveal his belief in pattern and movement toward a higher historical objective, his fellow historians were ever more critical of a history which was also a philosophy of history.

The British student of the rise and decline of civilizations was not, however, without his American defenders. Those who admired him usually did so for reasons which emphasized the necessity of viewing history in the larger perspective provided by Toynbee. Some were simply impressed by his display of knowledge and command of historical data. But underlying much of the appreciation was the belief that the historian of the postwar era would have to follow the trails which Toynbee had blazed if they were to maintain any position of influence and direction within society. Not only was Toynbee defended but, inescapably, metahistory had to be included in the mechanics of that defense.

Especially appealing to Toynbee protagonists was his insistence that historical study must embrace the totality of the historical experience in order to be instructive for modern times. The contemporary age with its sudden confrontation with the shrunken size of the planet and its new awareness of peoples and places once encountered only in romantic adventure tales or movie travelogues felt an instant empathy with the vision of a historian whose ken was similarly universal. Bewildered, confused, and frequently frustrated by the chaos of a world no longer intelligible on the old terms, the twentieth-century man discovered some hope in Toynbee that the individual was not completely helpless in the face of such staggering multiplicity, "a Toynbee appearing to gaze serenely across an infinite, but to him intelligible universe properly commands awe, admiration, and assured readership." The image was just as attractive to many historians. "Who experienced the shock of the limitless universality of our age as early and as deeply? Who has tried to cope as a historian, not with the tiny segment of the global chaos that falls within his competence but with the shock itself." Indeed, it was the shock of recognition that convinced some historians that a return to universal history, so long discredited, was the proper study of historians after all. One did not have to agree with all, or for that matter any, of Toynbee's interpretations or conclusions to agree with his approach, for the British historian had "made it inescapably clear that history is the study of all human experience, that its proper objective and only justification is the search for meaningful uniformities in the development of human societies."[2] That this kind of study might lead to blurred boundaries between history and philosophy and between history and religion was not only to be risked but also to be welcomed as necessity.

Even historians who found much to fault in Toynbee's massive study believed that his impact on the profession had been a healthy one. Geoffrey Bruun declared that Toynbee had "helped to rouse a myopic generation of historians from their dogmatic slumbers," and Crane Brinton said that the question, Whither Mankind? was worth exploring by all historians.[3] The great questions which have disturbed mankind since the birth of human consciousness and with which historians had once been so deeply involved could not be easily ignored or set aside. If Toynbee had accomplished nothing else, he had demonstrated the folly of any humanistic scholarship which denied the validity of asking such questions and essaying answers. His utilization of the comparative method criticized by so many had come to be accepted as a logical vehicle for ascertaining historical truth and as a fit companion for the fact finding of narrative

[2] Philip J. Wolfson, "Friedrich Meinecke (1862–1954)," *Journal of the History of Ideas*, Vol. XVII (October, 1956), 511; Von Laue, "Is There a Crisis in the Writing of History?" *Bucknell Review*, Vol. XLV (December, 1966), 3; Edward Whiting Fox, "History and Mr. Toynbee," *Virginia Quarterly Review*, Vol. XXXVI (Summer, 1960), 459.

[3] Geoffrey Bruun, "Challenge and Response," *Saturday Review*, (May 27, 1961), 16–17; Crane Brinton, review of Toynbee, *America and the World Revolution and Other Lectures*, in *American Historical Review*, Vol. LXVIII (April, 1963), 758–59.

history.[4] Toynbee's excursion into metahistory, his flirtation with theodicy, and his refusal to permit himself to be restricted by any artificial limitations decreed by either accepted practice or the legacy of scientific history established an example which others, more timidly, have followed. Historians have become less averse to trying to say what it all means.[5]

Those historians who have defended both Toynbee and the inclusion of metahistorical material as a legitimate part of the historian's purview have justified their claims with various arguments, ranging from the negative idea that, since somebody will write metahistory, it is better for the trained craftsman to attempt it to the more positive assertion that metahistory is an appropriate unit for historical study. But behind the several rationalizations has emerged a pattern which, in its ultimate implication and its philosophical suggestion, threatens to be as revolutionary and as far reaching as the historicism of the nineteenth century or the relativism of the twentieth. As of yet the number of adherents attracted to the banner of metahistory has been small, but their ranks appear to be increasing, and their influence within the profession to be growing.

At the simplest level of justification defenders of the Toynbeean approach to the study of history could point to those historians of the past whose works were still read and whose names remained familiar. Almost without exception those who had managed to say something which had retained any kind of significance over a long span of years were those who had attempted to extract some general meaning from their studies which was applicable to the human condition and which offered a measure of guidance and hope to beleaguered man. Great historians from Herodotus onward had been metahistorians in the finest sense of the word in that they had not just struggled to impart factual information but had also labored to suggest general truths as well.[6] Some, like Thucydides or Voltaire, did not move beyond the historical to the suprahistorical, but even

4 Rushton Coulborn, *The Origins of Civilized Societies, ix.*

5 Walter Prescott Webb, review of Geoffrey Barraclough, *History in a Changing World*, in *American Historical Review*, Vol. LXII (April, 1957), 595.

6 M. I. Finley, "Generalizations in Ancient History," in Gottschalk (ed.), *Generalization in the Writing of History*, 34.

they were aware of the moral and religious character implicit in their work. True, they did not develop schemes of historical cycles like Giambattista Vico or Bishop Bossuet, but they were most painfully aware that when the historian answered a question of interpretation arising legitimately from his research he would almost immediately be led further toward answering questions of a more ultimate nature. To explain the causes of a particular war, as, for example, Thucydides did in the case of the Peloponnesian conflict of the fifth century B.C., was only a prelude to generalizing not only about the causes of that war but also about the causes of all wars and, eventually, about the relationship of man to man, of man to fate, of man to God, and final destiny. The great historians understood this, and despite admitted excesses it was this very faculty which contributed so much to their greatness. The analogue was transparent: a return to concern with the great philosophical questions meant also a return to great historians.

There were also those who perceived the ferment going on around them in fields other than history—a ferment which only too frequently involved theorizing about the entire historical process. Many lamented the fact that a century of "scientific" historians had divorced themselves from any philosophical or metaphysical involvement. It was foolish to believe, some held, that just because the historian refused to engage in metahistorical speculation none would be undertaken. Moreover, the historian who maintained that theory did not enter his own work was guilty of obvious naïveté. "In the absence of any discussion of theory, history has often been influenced by a variety of undiscussed and unanalyzed theories . . . . By denying life to theory, history has often been dominated by theory's ghost." Would it not be much better for the historian to do his own theorizing, to attempt at least tentative answers to mankind's ancient and pressing questions? The historian could not isolate himself from what was occurring in other disciplines. Should he continue to do so, he might well succeed in abandoning a domain where he had special competence to the philosopher, the social scientist, and other modern soothsayers. "The task of interpreting history," claimed Wallace K. Ferguson, "is now more important than that of adding to the already unmanageable accumulation of factual material."[7] Yet it should not be assumed that the defenders of metahistory saw themselves only as simple guardians of the historical territory against the poaching of related studies. They were also very much convinced that the highest purpose of historical study was the acquisition of meaning; an insight into history was also an insight into the movement of life as well.

Friends of metahistory argued convincingly that Toynbee and his followers had not really demonstrated heresy by their concern with what lay beyond history or with their inquiry into the direction and flow of history toward that beyond. They insisted, rather, that it had been the historians of the "scientific" school who had perverted and distorted the nature of history and the role of the historian. "Historical research," avowed W. B. Willcox, "like any other form of curiosity, is a quest for meaning; and the historian is therefore by necessity a pattern-maker." The historian, consequently, was not prostituting his craft when he went beyond the limits of his factual material. Such limits had been self-imposed; they had not been ordained from on high. Indeed, there was no iron, inflexible, universal law which forbade the historian to consider the metaphysical implications of his work. The decline of historians, felt Richard Sullivan, was directly traceable to the allowing of so-called historical objectivity to "emasculate their minds before questions to which people demand answers." And answers could be provided without discarding the methodology of the "scientific" school. Lesley B. Simpson had early perceived the necessity of adding why to the traditional what. He had been willing to take the risk and had articulated the feelings of a growing number of historians when he said: "and, if that makes us philosophers, why, then, let's be philosophers as well."[8]

7 E. N. Peterson, "Historical Scholarship and World Unity," *Social Research*, Vol. XXVII (January, 1961), 449; Wallace K. Ferguson, review of Joseph R. Strayer (ed.), *The Interpretation of History*, in *American Historical Review*, Vol. XLIX (January, 1944), 262.

8 Willcox, "An Historian Looks at Social Change," in Eisenstadt (ed.), *The Craft of American History*, I, 31–32; Sullivan, "Toynbee's Debtors," *South Atlantic Quarterly*, Vol. LVIII (Winter, 1959), 80; Lesley B. Simpson, "Thirty Years of the Review," *Hispanic American Historical Review*, Vol. XXIX (May, 1949), 198.

A corollary to the postulate that the search for higher meaning was intrinsic to historical study was the observation that the historian dealt as much with the abstract and the invisible as he did with the concrete and the visible. Because his primary subject is man in all his relationships and metamorphoses, the historian cannot escape concerning himself with those values which his subjects esteem. If man himself is to be taken seriously (as assuredly the historian must), it follows that what man believes, what he is willing to fight and die for, what fantasies and dreams possess him must likewise be accorded a serious hearing. The historian can no more dichotomize the material from the nonmaterial than the physician can excise spirit from body. To omit from historical research consideration of those matters which have exercised the most profound influence upon human activity and which have forever been the foci of the deepest human thought and concern is to vitiate the very structure of history itself. Inevitably a refusal to contemplate metahistory, it was argued, led to the selfsame emasculation. A historian out of sympathy with the metahistorical in his own work could not be expected to empathize with the mystical longings of those about whom he wrote. The great defect of historical training was that it did not equip the student to deal with those forces which could not be measured.[9]

The manner in which the historian generally has handled the matter of religious experience provides a useful example. So much of history is the product of man's search for faith that no historian can avoid the issue without doing violence to historical substance. It would, perhaps, not be too extreme to state that the single largest influencing factor on human development has been religion. Consequently, any history which fails to comprehend the importance of religious and quasi-religious ideas to human experience can never penetrate the mysteries of motivation and behavior. But because religion usually manifests itself through incorporeal means and because historical methodology is unprepared to admit evidence of such insubstantial nature, written history usually is unsuccessful in

9 Kenneth S. Latourette, "The Christian Understanding of History," *American Historical Review*, Vol. LIV (January, 1949), 270.

recapturing the dynamism of a past so frequently dominated by religious passion and prejudice. Trained to deal with the concreteness of ascertainable fact, distilled from documents, papers, and reports, the historian has often found himself unable to portray vividly those things which are not found precisely in written sources and which involve an understanding of that side of human behavior which is at once transcendent and often illogical. Many historians would be eager to dismiss as unimportant that which they find irrational, unprovable, or smacking of myth. But these things have been terribly real to men in the past, and experience suggests that they are likely to remain so in the future.

Can one understand the dynamics of Hebrew history without seeing the Biblical Jehovah through the eyes of the ancient Israelites? The reality, to the Jews, of the covenant with Abraham and Moses, of the dramatic exodus from Egypt, and the idea of a promised land and a chosen people are factors which the historian of ancient times disregards at the peril of historical failure. Can the motivating power which spurred the Crusades be adequately explained solely in terms of economic desire and dynastic rivalry? Can the actions of any of the Protestant reformers or the Catholic counter-reformers be satisfactorily comprehended upon any base which does not take into account the reality of religious belief and heritage? And, in discussing the extremes of religious behavior, whether it be the Anabaptists of the sixteenth century in Europe or the Millerites of nineteenth-century America waiting expectantly for the end of the world in white robes atop the hills of Massachusetts, historians have been even further bewildered. Extremes are dutifully pictured as hysterical aberrations or at best as bizarre practices providing anecdotal material for lecture or book but hardly revealing meaningful insight into the historical mainstream. The historian must take as seriously these beliefs of men as they themselves did. Otherwise his history will be neither truthful nor, in the best sense, history.[10] An awareness of the preoccupation of mankind with religion and ultimate destiny should persuade the historian that for him to pursue a similar drive

[10] Theodore M. Green, "A Philosophical Appraisal of the Christian Interpretation of History," *Pacific Historical Review*, XXVI (May, 1957), 130.

by asking himself what it all means is not incompatible with his historianship. It may well be a natural outgrowth.

It was not enough, however, to justify metahistory on the grounds that men within history pursued other worldly or supernatural goals. While an understanding of this aspect of human behavior might well enhance the historian's ability to re-create with more accuracy a particular historical situation, it did not necessarily justify the historian's quest for meaning in the suprahistorical. Or, on a more pragmatic level, just because a yearning public demanded the solace of discovering meaning, direction, and a unity of action in history did not mean that the historian was compelled to placate the demand. The validity of metahistory demanded firmer foundations, and a few historians since 1945 have conceived a basis rooted in the metaphysics of history which argued the efficacy of metahistory.

The best expression of this view was formulated by Hans Kohn. Arguing that an inner contradiction first had to be accepted, Kohn maintained that it was impossible for any man, historian or otherwise, to place himself outside history. "We are always in it." But the perception of unity in history results in historical transcendence inasmuch as such perception is not history. The act of detecting unity and pattern is not a historical act but a spiritual decision. "Thus history itself becomes the way to the suprahistorical to which there leads no road but through history."[11] Under this interpretation the road traveled by Toynbee was not only the correct one; it was the only one. Unlike previous historical philosophers who superimposed a pattern of unity obtained from outside of history, Toynbee in the Kohn model discerned his pattern from within the framework of history itself. Metahistory, then, becomes not the product of religion or philosophy or ideology but the natural result of historical vision within history. The capstone of all historical research becomes metahistory—the logical end of historical labor and the primary justification for historical study.

11 Hans Kohn, review of Karl Jaspers, *Vom Ursprung und Ziel der Geschicte*, in *American Historical Review*, Vol. LVI (January, 1951), 328. See also Kohn's statement on universal history in "A Historian's Creed for Our Time," *South Atlantic Quarterly*, Vol. LII (July, 1953), 342.

It would be fair to assume that not many practicing historians have yet embraced the idea of metahistory. It still remains somewhat beyond the boundary of scholarly respectability, and few historians possess either the inclination or the training to advance its cause. Yet, surprisingly, a number of historical writers have begun to acknowledge its presence and even to suggest that it might be valuable for all historians.

The principal gain envisaged has to do with the quality of mind of the historian himself. In order for any writer of history to retain that facet of creative imagination which distinguishes the truly innovative historian from his more prosaic counterparts, he must constantly keep himself open to new suggestions, to stretch his mind in directions which may at times be uncomfortable and unfamiliar. Certainly, metahistory accomplishes this. Any scheme of system building based on a measurement of historical currents and forces requires concentration, wide knowledge, and a willingness to confront the speculative. H. Stuart Hughes has suggested that metahistorians "are the writers who actually operate on the *frontiers* of historical thinking" and believes that imaginative hypotheses developed on the metahistorical level "offer the indispensable raw material for subsequent criticism and elaboration." Crane Brinton urged his professional colleagues to try "something close to philosophical history" without losing the "virtues of the scientific attitude." These were significant concessions and an implicit acknowledgment of Toynbee's influence upon the profession.[12]

What has been described in this chapter, it should be admitted, has not been a primary trend in postwar historical thought, if that determination is to be computed in terms of numbers. There is little evidence that historians in America are being converted to the Toynbeean approach or that very many have bestowed much more than a passing comment upon the entire field. What seems especially significant, however, is that there has been any trend at all. This is at once revealing and revolutionary in its implications. Such concern,

---

[12] Hughes, "The Historian and the Social Scientist," *American Historical Review,* Vol. LXVI (October, 1960), 27; Brinton, "Many Mansions," *American Historical Review*, Vol. LXIX (January, 1964), 319.

however modest its beginnings, reflects the larger concerns of society and reveals that not all historians are willing to eliminate from their work the larger questions of existence. Moreover, a willingness to embark once again upon the search for unifying historical themes, to view history as pattern, and to suspect the pervasiveness of historical purpose represents a sharp break with the bequest of "scientific" history. This does not have to mean, as so many have feared, a return to the determinism of previous patternmakers who had particular religious or ideological axes to grind; it could well mean a search for unity and meaning within the historical framework, offering perhaps some comfort and assurance in an age which has seen so many certainties obliterated. Should historians choose to reassert their oneness with humanity and to place their craft at its service, they would go far in reclaiming their premier position among the humanities.[13]

[13] There have been many opponents of this view. Two of the best statements opposing any flirtation with metahistory are Savelle, "The Philosophy of the General: Toynbee versus the Naturalists," *Pacific Historical Review*, Vol. XXV (February, 1956), 66; and William O. Aydelotte, "Notes on Historical Generalization," in Gottschalk (ed.), *Generalization in the Writing of History*, 155.

In the years following the uneasy peace of 1945, historians have given renewed attention not only to the nature of their craft and its relationship to the crisis of the contemporary world but also to the historian himself and those particular qualities of mind which it is felt should characterize historical work. Obviously, if one were able to put together a composite historian from the pastiches of what writers have decided are desirable attributes, one would have the perfect historian. And perfection among historians is as rare as it is in any other field. Two years before the war ended, Richard Shyrock described this mythical man as one who combined complete scientific research with great literary artistry.[1] Shyrock believed that such historians were so infrequently encountered that they did not merit much practical consideration. Yet, if it is true that the "perfect" historian is not available, it still is not unreasonable to demand that the virtues associated with him be cultivated individually by less exalted writers of history. What is revealing about the self-examination undertaken by historians in America in the past generation is the kind of quality most often emphasized as being especially vital to the present time. What has occurred has been a wedding of the relativist critique of the 1930's with an existentialism produced by the tragedy of World War II and its aftermath. The result has been a reorientation of values in the determination of what constitutes the true historian.

Essential to this analysis of historianship was the realization of how strikingly similar was the historian within the context of his professional work to the individual entrapped in the confines of an

[1] Richard H. Shyrock, "American Historiography: A Critical Analysis and a Program," American Philosophical Society *Proceedings*, Vol. LXXXVII (1943), 40.

amoral society and a neutral universe. They were both alone, and nothing could substantially alleviate that basic loneliness. Written history could not successfully be the product of a team or a group. "History worthy of being read has to be based on information gathered, pondered, and digested by a single mind, written by a single hand."[2] The historian's rendering of the past was a personal project which came into existence only after it had been filtered through the screen of his own experience and mental outlook. It was not a task which could be delegated, not something which could be shared except on the most superficial level. Even the completed history usually afforded its readers only a momentary and fleeting glimpse into the agony and thought which had produced it. Just as the individual in an Albert Camus novel must provide for himself whatever morality and significance is to be found in life, so the historian must do the same thing for his history. And, in both cases, it is a task which must be performed alone.

It is this approximation of the human condition in his professional life which should impart to the historian a natural insight into the tragic dimensions of existence and allow him, better than other observers, to give his art a realism and poignancy which goes beyond the simple recording of past people and events. The sense of tragedy, a feeling for the bittersweet taste of life, has always been present in the writings of the great historians; one suspects that it is because of these qualities that they have been remembered. One cannot read Thucydides' account of the plague in Athens or Thomas Carlyle's description of the dark forces unleashed by the French Revolution seen in the carts rolling to the guillotine or William H. Prescott's magnificent recounting of the march of Hernán Cortes upon Tenochtitlán on his way to destroy a civilization without recognizing the epic proportions of human tragedy. But historians who have been forced to come to terms with the unspeakable reality of the nuclear age have had their sense of tragedy sharpened, their awareness of catastrophe unbearably clarified, and their vision of ultimate apocalypse made to seem terribly imminent. Under such circum-

2 W. T. Laprade, "Obstacles in Studying History," *South Atlantic Quarterly*, Vol. LIX (Spring, 1960), 206.

stances it is not surprising that historians came to see that any history which captured an audience, which spoke meaningfully in contemporary times, had to be one in which the writer felt both understanding and partnership with its victims. In short, the historian had to become as involved in history as were those whom he described.[3] Ironically, that quality which was now being demanded of historians was one which relativists like Carl Becker and Charles Beard a generation before had argued was an unavoidable facet of historiography.

The relativists, in denouncing the claims of "scientific" history to the possibility of an objective history, made two basic assumptions: one about the nature of history and the other about the nature of the historian. Concerning the former they asserted that the past was not capturable in any complete sense. Only fragments remained, and whatever story was pieced together by the historian was, of necessity, fragmentary. Any claim to totality, therefore, was absurd. Moreover, even if enough historical records were discovered to provide a fairly comprehensive picture of some event or figure, there was no assurance that could be given to the historian that the records revealed reality. The relativist thinkers, greatly influenced by an age of psychology, were very much aware that the printed or spoken word was not always a reliable indicator of truth. To the critics of scientific history, then, neither the quantity of records nor the records themselves were satisfactory guarantees of objective history.

Even more serious were relativist objections to the role of historian as objective researcher, as neutral scientist. Claiming that the writer of history could not escape his own system of value judgments and moral preconceptions, the relativists maintained that the truly scientific historian was myth and that those who maintained they were scientific were self-deluded. All history had to come through a particular person's mind, and that mind was not comparable to the sterile vessels of the laboratory. It was bound to shape and color the final product. In essence that is what Carl Becker meant when he said that everyman was his own historian. "Written history," said Charles Beard, "was an act of faith," more akin to a

[3] Smith, *The Historian and History*, 230–31.

Kierkegaardian leap of affirmation than to the precise formulas of a laboratory report. Relativism stressed the historian as participant, as within history himself, and unable to play the role of detached observer. What the existential situation demanded was that historians not only recognize this reality but welcome it. It was demanded that the historian be a participant as well as a recorder. The marriage of relativism and existentialism, alluded to earlier, was an unconscious ceremony but clearly visible in a cluster of qualities which historians deemed desirable for themselves after 1945.

Accepting the relativist idea that bias was inescapable in historical writing,[4] historians suggested that this "vice" of scientific history might actually become a "virtue." Practically all historians now admitted that prejudice and the writer's own preconceptions were going to be present in any historical work. Why not construct a *conscious* philosophy of history since an *unconscious* one would manifest itself in any event? Edward N. Saveth pointed out that the conscious use of hypotheses did not necessarily make a work any less prejudiced than those which contained pledges of impartiality in their prefaces.[5] Furthermore, by affirming without any equivocation an avowed purpose or scheme of presentation, the writer was putting the reader on notice and allowing him to formulate objections openly without forcing him to tilt at hidden windmills, all the more insidious because of their subtlety. An open confession of a conceptual frame of reference would dissipate some of the fog which usually enveloped written history, especially when it was claimed that only the facts were being presented. Carl Becker earlier had

4 Practically every kind of historian in every age group accepted the idea that bias was always present in historical writing. For some representative statements see the following: William J. Grace, "Jacques Maritain and Modern Catholic Historical Scholarship," *Journal of the History of Ideas*, Vol. V (October, 1944), 434; Bernard A. Weisberger, "The Dark and Bloody Ground of Reconstruction Historiography," *Journal of Southern History*, Vol. XXV (November, 1959), 446; Samuel F. Bemis, "First Gun of a Revisionist Historiography for the Second World War," *Journal of Modern History*, Vol. XIX (March, 1947), 55; and Howard K. Beale, "The Professional Historian: His Theory and Practice," *Pacific Historical Review*, Vol. XXII (August, 1953), 243.

5 Edward N. Saveth, "A Science of American History," in Eisenstadt (ed.), *The Craft of American History*, I, 126–27.

generally demolished the idea that historical facts had an independent objectivity. Most had come to agree with Herbert Weisinger that "a fact is not a fact because it is a raw piece of information, whatever that might mean, but because it is a recognizable part of a scheme of interpretation into which it fits."[6]

What, of course, had to be admitted was that written history was innately subjective. And this was an admission which few academically trained historians were willing to make. Graduate-school experience buttressed by a century of assertions that history should strive for accuracy and objective truth made the notion of subjectivity in history appear unscholarly and dangerous. There was much precedent to recommend the latter view. The past was replete with examples of the subversion of history in order to support or denigrate a particular cause or philosophy. Nations had employed historians to justify a foreign policy, as in the case of World War I. The seeking out of only those facts which fit a self-serving hypothesis or system was a readily apparent sin of many historians. But this kind of subjectivity was not what was being requested. A confusion in terms and their meanings was to a large degree responsible for the seeming irreparable breach between the two schools of thought. The misunderstanding stemmed largely from a confusing of subjectivity with partiality and a corresponding tendency to equate objectivity with impartiality. Subjectivity did not necessarily imply inaccuracy or untruth. The historian who deliberately sets out to deceive his readers is guilty of the lowest kind of unethical practice, and no one would argue otherwise.[7] But the historian may fulfill his obligation to accuracy and at the same time be subjective if subjectivity in history is defined as it should be, namely, that written history is an artistic creation, manufactured by the writer in much the same way that a novelist creates a novel or a dramatist a play. Since the finished product is a human creation, there can be little doubt about its basic

[6] Herbert Weisinger, "Ideas of History During the Renaissance," *Journal of the History of Ideas*, Vol. VI (October, 1945), 415.

[7] A very good statement concerning the historian's obligation to be as accurate as possible may be found in Peter Masten Dunne, "The Renaissance and the Reformation: A Study in Objectivity (Legends Black and White)," *Pacific Historical Review*, Vol. XXVI (May, 1957), 121.

subjectivity.[8] It has been molded, shaped, tinted, and forged through the mind and experience of the historian. This does not make it any the less truthful or meaningful. Indeed, it may make it more so, for if the historian is to acquire that relevancy which seems so highly prized today, it will not be through recourse to the objectivity of his data but rather through his ability to say something about the universality of the human experience. And that ability will depend very much on his reclamation of a subjectivity which spurns the bitterness of partisanship while yet embracing the passion of involvement.

In thinking and writing about the nature of professional qualifications historians have, since the end of World War II made the kind of subjectivity described above one of the attributes they feel most desirable in themselves. Around this idea of an emotional humanism they have also grouped other characteristics which reflect much the same attitude, one which emphasizes the historian's concern rather than his aloofness. The demand has been that the historian feel as well as think, that he grasp what it means to make choices, that he formulate his hypotheses and systems as much through intuition as through logic. In short, there has been a demand for the historian to become more human so that his history becomes more alive.

One aspect of that humanity which historians since the onset of scientific historiography have traditionally scorned has been the making of judgments and the building of a world view through intuitive insight rather than by a process of induction. Most regarded intuition as an unreliable device which smacked too much of the mystical and the illogical. The fact that most people in conducting their everyday lives more often than not operated from a less scientific basis, that people often *felt* the rightness or wrongness of things, was dismissed as irrelevant to the function of the historian. Recent American historical thought, however, shaken both by the critique of the relativists and by dissatisfaction with the inability of scientific historiography to make good on its promises, has re-examined the idea of intuition as a means of arriving at historical truth

8 R. F. Arragon, "History's Changing Image: With Such Permanence as Time Has," *American Scholar*, Vol. XXXIII (Spring, 1964), 226.

and has concluded that its possession is an indispensable quality for the historian.

It would be a mistake, however, to assume that those who advocated a reliance upon intuition believed that the writer of history simply sat down in his study, bereft of records or research materials, and through some occult process of divination fashioned his history. There was no thought that the painstaking and time-consuming activities commonly associated with historical research be abandoned. No one argued that the historian dispense with a reliance upon facts and sources or that he become a fabricator in the mold of the storyteller—only that he not ignore the insight of intuition at certain critical junctures in his work.

At some point in his research and writing, it was argued, the historian reaches a point where, in order to make intelligible his mass of data, he must, himself, be able to see through his records to the pattern. What is essentially an artistic creation has to reveal at these points the hand of the creator. Perhaps this would not be necessary if the historian could be sure that all the records pertinent to his study were available or if he could be positive that he had cleansed himself of all bias and preference. But since he can be sure of neither, his only choice is to rely upon his own intuitive grasp of the matter under study to guide him. To be sure, his intuition is an informed one, aided immeasurably by his own scrutiny of the documents, by his own immersion into the nuances of the past, and by his own personal experience. Yet his presentation is intuitive in that the final picture he portrays for his readers has been accomplished without the benefit of mathematical certitude, regardless of how many footnotes adorn his conclusions.

The nature of the historian's intuitive capacity has been described in various ways. Arthur M. Schlesinger, Jr., compared it to the "diagnostic judgments of the doctor," suggesting that, as he studies history, the historian develops a "sense of what is possible in human affairs, derived from a feeling for the continuities and discontinuities of existence." Lynn White, Jr., observed that "the historian must create his patterns of probable truth less in terms of specific records and more in terms of relationships intuitively evident to him as he deals with the records."[9] It seems to be an extraordinarily subtle process, one incapable of being broken down into its component parts for dissection. This probability lends truth to the claim that the historian is actually involved in a distinctive act of creation. And philosophers and psychologists have long been frustrated in attempts to comprehend and then explain the mechanics of creation as it relates to the poet or the painter. Indeed, a good many historians have maintained in recent years that the task of the historian is more closely related to the novelist than it is to the scientist and that those qualities which make for success in fictional literature are similarly commendable in the historian.[10] Certainly, one of these qualities is the capacity for intuition.

The intuitive role seems to be most significant in interpretative history; it is both in the formulation of hypothesis and in the manufacture of synthesis that the work of the historian most closely approximates that of the artist. Harold P. Simonson explored this relationship in an extremely perceptive article written in 1964 in which he used Frederick Jackson Turner's frontier thesis as a case in point. Simonson contended that the reason for the popularity of the idea was Turner's perception of "a mythical quality which raised his account far above mere factual description." Citing Paul Tillich's *Interpretation of History* as supporting argument, Simonson went to the crucial point: that the writing of interpretative history "demands of the historian an artist's mythical consciousness to interpret the materials at hand in symbolic terms."[11] This was Turner's great accomplishment, or, for that matter, the accomplishment of any historian who gives us a new and different way of looking at something. It does not lessen the accomplishment appreciably to admit that the view of reality presented is but one view, or even to confess

[9] Arthur M. Schlesinger, Jr., "On the Inscrutability of History," *Encounter*, Vol. XXVII (November, 1966), 11; Lynn White, Jr., "The Changing Past," *Harper's*, Vol. CCIX (November, 1954), 32.

[10] George V. Taylor, "History, Literature and the Public at Large," *North Carolina Historical Review*, Vol. XLII (April, 1965), 188; Higham in Higham et al., *History*, 141.

[11] Harold P. Simonson, "Frederick Jackson Turner: Frontier History as Art," *Antioch Review*, Vol. XXIV (Summer, 1964), 211.

that the view presented may be distorted one way or another, may be subject to modification and revision as it is tested by the work of later scholars. It is still an authentic view in that its meaning depends in no small measure upon what it says to a present readership about its own sense of historical identity. The mythic element in history stretches both backward and forward in time. The sense of the myth, arrived at more or less intuitively, is one of the historian's most necessary qualities. Those who have possessed it abundantly we have classified as great.

If intuition is defined as creative hypothesis, an analogy between the historian and the physical scientist can also be clearly seen. It is not just the artist or the novelist who arrives at truth through a process which involves subjective perception. Frequently discoveries in science have been precipitated by hypotheses which still lacked sufficient data for proof. Einstein's theories of relativity and Darwin's explanation for the origin of species are good examples of ideas which were expressed before all the evidence was visible. The historian who in looking at the prism of history glimpses a new refraction is not so different from the scientist who proposes a theory of optics or genetics because he intuitively feels it to be true. The use of intuition by the historian has parallels in both art and science.

All great historians likewise have contained within their writing the quality of imagination—an attribute closely akin to the faculty of intuition but different from it in a number of subtle ways. Imagination in historical writing refers more precisely to the ability to reconstruct in one's own mind a picture of the past and to translate the vividness and living imagery of that portrait to the printed page. The famous Dutch historian Johan Huizinga defined it as well as anyone. He called it "the chief historical talent" and "that image-making force which recreates an original thing so that others may seem to see the features and hear the voices of the billions of people who have lived."[12] The use of imagination does not imply the employment of "made-up" facts or the inclusion of artificial "imaginings," but rather it indicates the ability of the historian to bring back

12 J. Huizinga, "History Changing Form," *Journal of the History of Ideas*, Vol. IV (April, 1943), 217.

to life a past that no longer exists. This goal can only be attained through a series of steps which, taken together, can be termed imaginative reconstruction. Since the historian as a contemporary person cannot literally live in the past, he must do the next best thing: bring the past to the present. It is imagination which allows him to do so. Without imagination the historian brings back only dead fragments, like pieces of ancient exotic pottery, to a present which more than likely will ignore the offering. In deciding upon those qualities which should be a part of the perfect historian, postwar writers have consistently placed imagination at the head of their lists.

It is, of course, much easier to identify imaginative historical writing than it is to say what exactly is missing in a history where the ingredient is lacking. That is undoubtedly because imagination is not a single thing. It is not just the use of appropriate adjectives and adverbs; it is not simply relating how an individual felt at a certain crucial time, as, say, when Robert E. Lee ordered his troops forward at Gettysburg or when Napoleon marched into Moscow. It is all these things and more. It is being able to catch in words the motion of life, of a society, of a time in the past. It is a motion picture rather than a still life. It blends together enough of the details and idiosyncrasies of a past time to show not only its individual character but also its very breathing. It captures within its light the subtlety of change as well as the concreteness of permanence.[13] What appears to be its basic component is its imparting of vitality—the re-creation of life. Many different kinds of writers have displayed it, from Herodotus to Samuel Eliot Morison, and so there is no single literary method which can be prescribed. Obviously, however, historical imagination is not something which can be turned on or off at will. It requires constant use to remain fresh. The historian has to work at stretching his imagination; he must constantly subject his word pictures to its demands. Otherwise, it will atrophy and die.

The relationship of imagination to good historical writing has

[13] Allan Nevins emphasizes this kind of imagination in "History This Side the Horizon," in Eisenstadt (ed.), *The Craft of American History*, II, 262.

been recognized by a number of historians and others who have been interested in history. The major American figure in the neo-orthodox religious movement, Reinhold Niebuhr, who found in the study of history the ingredients of tragedy, believed that the historian "must have artistic imagination to discern the dramatic pattern which is spelled out by the facts." Richard W. Van Alstyne, whose lifetime has been devoted to the study of American diplomatic history, maintained that "a good historian can do better with only a few facts than a poor one with many." And the reason cited by Van Alstyne was that "the quality of his [the historian's] product is determined by the extent of his imaginative powers." George Kennan discovered that when he turned from diplomacy to the writing of history that "the describing of historical events . . . was partly an act of the creative imagination of the writer . . . . To arrive at its true significance . . . you had to put yourself in the place of the people who were there."[14] The exercise of imagination, then, is a most necessary quality for the modern historian, and the contemporary emphasis upon its importance reveals once again a sharp break with some of the strictures of scientific historiography. Combined with the confession of bias and the utilization of intuition, historical imagination forms a trinity of virtues now found desirable in writers of history and reflects the great conceptual change engendered by the crisis of our times.

Most historians have also made readability or literary artistry one of the qualities they consider mandatory for the "perfect" historian. Yet the feeling persists that many are doing little more than paying lip service to one of those commonly accepted ideals that nobody takes very seriously. Since history is written, it would be the height of ludicrousness to ask that it be written badly. Urging that history be readable and artistically acceptable falls, then, into the same

[14] Reinhold Niebuhr, "Is History Predictable?" *Atlantic*, Vol. CXCIV (July, 1954), 69; Richard W. Van Alstyne, "History and the Imagination," *Pacific Historical Review*, Vol. XXXIII (February, 1964), 11; Kennan, "The Experience of Writing History," *Virginia Quarterly Review*, Vol. XXXVI (Spring, 1960), 207. See also the comments of William H. McNeill, "Some Basic Assumptions of Toynbee's *A Study of History*," in Edward T. Gorgan (ed.), *The Intent of Toynbee's History*, 41.

category as the flag and motherhood. And about as much attention has been paid to homilies about good writing as is usually given to political clichés concerning "Old Glory" and the beauties of American family life. Historians have consistently agreed that history was written to be read and just as consistently turned out a persistent stream of one dull monograph after another. But the question of whether history is also good literature involves a much more profound matter than frequent admonitions about writing skill. It involves the very heart of the historian's art and has been recently the topic of vigorous discussion.

The ancient question whether history is art or science requires definition and will be considered in the next chapter; however, in determining the most sought-after qualities in the historian, writers have emphasized the relationship between the historian and his literary brothers, the novelist and the dramatist. This has been especially true of those who see the function of the historian to be closely associated with narrative history.[15] In any type of narrative, fictional or historical, its impact upon the audience, the core of its appeal, depends in large measure upon its ability to achieve the dramatic. In other words, it must tell a story that has plot, characterization, suspense, and a climax which is aesthetically satisfactory. Narrative history can no more defy these conventions and be successful than can the novel or the play. If there is one theme which appears recurrently in the postwar period, it is the theme of history as dramatic art. From the gifted amateur, like Bernard De Voto, to the academic professional, like John D. Hicks, the sermon has been the same: good history is dramatic history.[16]

While it may be argued that history itself is an art, there can be little debate that the writing of history constitutes an artistic endeavor.[17] The historian meets all the same problems and has to answer all the same questions that confront any other writer. His

---

[15] See pp. 32–55.

[16] Bernard De Voto, "The Easy Chair," *Harper's*, Vol. CXCVIII (April, 1949), 52–55; John D. Hicks, review of Arthur M. Schlesinger, Jr., *The Crisis of the Old Order*, in *American Historical Review*, Vol. LXIII (October, 1957), 157. An excellent article demonstrating the similarity between historian and dramatist is Loren Baritz, "The Historian as Playwright," *Nation*, November 24, 1962, p. 341.

finished product may or may not be accurate and reliable history, but it will always stand as a work of human creation—a work of art. Moreover, its chances of being read, of exercising a beneficent influence within society will depend greatly upon its appeal to the reading public. If history is to perform those functions which thoughtful historians have assigned it, it must be read. The ability to write, to organize material dramatically, and to entrap the reader with words becomes not only a literary nicety but also a practical necessity for the historian. To assure himself of the truth of this he need only recall that

> History in general would seem to be a form of literature hardly less ephemeral than journalism. Only a very select body of its practitioners has achieved immortality, and of this body it may be said without hesitation that in every instance they owed their distinction to the fruitful marriage of scholarship and art.[18]

For most historians the effort to incorporate an aesthetic structure into their writing would have to be a conscious one. They would have to return to some of the techniques used by the romantic historians of a century before.[19] Theme, atmosphere, and characterization would all have to be recultivated. This did not mean that it was also necessary to duplicate the excesses of romantic historiography or to subscribe to the many biases and ill-conceived notions which so often infiltrated their work. One can admire the drama inherent in the confrontation of civilizations as Prescott presented it in *The Conquest of Mexico* and *The Conquest of Peru* without agreeing with the subtle racism which is also a part of the volumes. One can appreciate the epic struggle of the Protestant Netherlands for independence from Catholic Spain as John L. Motley did in *The Rise of the Dutch Republic* without subscribing to Motley's anti-Catholicism. And one can appreciate the heroic activities of Montcalm and Wolfe so expertly described by Francis Parkman without coming

17 Samuel Eliot Morison, *By Land and By Sea: Essays and Addresses*, 289.

18 Ferdinand Schevill, "Ranke: Rise, Decline, and Persistence of a Reputation," *Journal of Modern History*, Vol. XXIV (September, 1952), 233–34.

19 Arthur Schlesinger, Jr., "The Historian as Artist," *Atlantic*, Vol. CCXII (July, 1963), 35–41.

to believe that heroes count for all. What the romantics understood was structure and dramatic form, and they were unashamed to utilize that knowledge to the fullest in their histories. Imitation was in order. One of the more important qualities demanded of historians was that their writing style be "not that of an expert speaking to specialists but that of a man speaking to men."[20]

The key quality, it would seem, which historians envisioned in their "perfect" historian was humanity. In a very significant sense what most were saying in the aftermath of World War II was that, for history to reclaim its lost audience and to recapture its public relevance, the historian must abandon his pose of scientific observer for the more dangerous role of fellow human being. He was not being asked to shed his solicitude for facts or his concern for truth; he was being asked only to be fully a man when he wrote his history. He should not just write from the detachment of a neutral observer but should enter into and share with his subjects their triumphs and tragedies. This approach would require him to see people as people, not as abstractions, and it would compel him to take sides when a serious moral issue was presented to him. He was being asked to respond to historical situations as a decent, civilized man, as well as a historian.

Allan Nevins warned the membership of the American Historical Association in 1960 of the dangers to history when it became dehumanized: "that instead of dissecting impersonal forces or presenting those misty wraiths the economic man or sociological man, the historian should narrate the past in terms of living men and women."[21] If the historian took Nevins' instruction seriously, he too had to be cognizant of his own individuality while not forgetting the commonality he shared with those he was describing. He had to consider sympathetically the aspirations and problems of the people he encountered in history, for in so doing he was demonstrating his own human capabilities. One of the reasons why psychology enjoyed

[20] Howard M. Jones, "The Nature of Literary History," *Journal of the History of Ideas*, Vol. XXVIII (April–June, 1967), 158.

[21] Allan Nevins, "Not Capulets, Not Montagues," *American Historical Review*, Vol. LXV (January, 1960), 258–59. A good statement on the role of the individual historian is found in A. S. Eisenstadt, *Charles McLean Andrews*, 220–21.

such status and reputation in contemporary society was that people tended to identify its practitioners with those who aimed at doing something helpful for a suffering humanity. Freudian terms might be a source of innumerable examples of barracks humor, but certainly psychoanalysis was widely recognized as a way in which people beset with trouble could be attended. The man Freud seemed to Richard L. Schoenwald to offer to historians a proper subject for emulation. The virtues he attributed to Freud, "a mind devoted to understanding, a heart not blocked and dead, an openness to new ideas, a sympathy that gives insight and a refusal to stop and despair," were ones that he suggested as desirable to historians as well.[22] These characteristics, it is true, would be admirable in any man, but they seemed particularly important for historians caught up in the great task of explaining to their fellow men the way the world had come to be. They could not forget that they too were living in that same world, equal victims of its injustices and caprice.

Nor could historians ignore their own personal system of values. In fact, a system of values which refracted the best of civilized behavior was an imperative in the list of qualifications drawn up by historians in the postwar re-examination. Since the historian was constantly called upon in his labors to make judgments and to call for an accounting of stewardship from those he studied, it was logically requisite that he have a firm and elevated base from which to operate. His values should not take the form of inflexible dogma, for "the historian is forced by the very nature of history constantly to review human values."[23] But a feeling for what was right, decent, and just and, quite as importantly, a respect for the value systems of others were essential. Indeed, one of the major deficiencies noted among recent graduate students in history was that "they lack personal values or philosophy." This was attributed by the critic to a lack of wide reading in the humanities, but whatever the reason

22 Richard L. Schoenwald, "Historians and the Challenge of Freud," *Western Humanities Review*, Vol. X (Spring, 1956), 108.

23 Bert James Loewenberg, "Some Problems Raised by Historical Relativism," *Journal of Modern History*, Vol. XXI (March, 1949), 23.

the indictment was a serious one.[24] For if the historian is to function freely and without pressure from either the state or any other agency, he must have a philosophy which holds certain ideals as fundamental —ideals which he is willing to defend. In a twentieth century which had already witnessed so many assaults upon the idea of free inquiry, in which the strands of rationality and humaneness were seen to be so desperately fragile, the historian had, at least, to be committed to a pattern of belief which held human freedom dear. His own survival was at stake.

The forging of a new composite of the "perfect" historian, a synthesis which emphasized certain qualities once deemed inimical to sound historical scholarship, did not, at the same time, eliminate many of the virtues associated with the older version. Many of the more traditional ideas about what constituted a good historian persisted in historical thought after 1945. This fact, by itself perhaps, testified to a long-accepted notion of historians: change is a gradual process, and any given situation will contain old as well as new elements. Of the more customary qualities which received mention, the most frequently cited were balance, humility, and integrity.

The word balance is a difficult one to define in any precise way as it applies to the writing of history. It is almost simpler to say what it does not mean: it does not mean impartiality, in the sense that the historian refuses to make judgments or come to conclusions; it does not mean that all sides or facets of a situation be totally explored, for this would be in many instances an intellectual impossibility; and it does not mean that the historian has to develop enough competence in myriad tangential fields before he can write accurate and successful history. Samuel Eliot Morison perhaps came the nearest to evoking its meaning for historians when he compared its meaning to that found in the French word *mesure*. Equating balance with proportion, Morison identified the quality as containing the capacity for open-mindedness, a willingness to see beyond the narrow spectrum of one's own field or area of research. It was, he

24 James H. Rodabaugh, "Historical Societies: Their Magazines and Their Editors," *Wisconsin Magazine of History*, Vol. XLV (Winter, 1961–62), 123.

felt, a *sine qua non* for the great or even the good historian.[25] It was
not something which could be acquired in a graduate seminar or by
reading a manual on historical method, for it was a cast of mind
rather than a learned response. But that it was a historian's necessity
most agreed.

Balance is likewise linked with the whole concept of perspective,
which has been discussed earlier as one of the functions of history.
Perspective is likely to contribute to a historian's sense of balance.
Indeed, one of the more ominous developments in modern historiography is that perspective has become increasingly endangered
by the knowledge explosion which has affected history as well as
scientific and technological fields. "The broadening of historical
knowledge has been accomplished by a narrowing of the historian's
view, in too many instances, to a small segment of history."[26] If,
then, the acquisition of balance is no longer attainable through a
broadening of perspective that automatically came with the study
of history, the answer to the problem might well be solved through
J. H. Hexter's declaration that " 'he also serves,' who sometimes
sits and thinks."[27]

The possession of balance would appear to be a prerequisite for
attitudes of humility and integrity. Without the former it is unlikely
that the latter qualities would be found. For humility comes from an
intellectual awareness of both the scope and the complexity of
knowledge, and integrity from a willingness to see the truth as
clearly as the evidence will permit. In an age when arrogance is so
often a substitute for wisdom and in which the sanity of balance is
frequently superseded by the strident rhetoric of partisanship and
special pleading, humility and integrity become even more propitious
and less often encountered among historians. "Historians," said
Wayne S. Cole, "need to emphasize the limits of their knowledge as
well as the expansiveness of it." Cole further urged historians to
cultivate the humility personified by an Albert Einstein, though he

[25] Morison, "Faith of a Historian," *American Historical Review*, Vol. LVI
(January, 1951), 262–69.
[26] Ferguson, *The Renaissance in Historical Thought*, 387.
[27] Hexter, *Reappraisals in History*, 43–44.

cautioned that "perhaps in the furious twentieth-century struggle for man's minds there can be no real place for moderation and restraint—even in historical interpretation." J. G. Randall hoped that historians would come to recognize that "historical competence comes only by long study, training, craftmanship, and experience" and that poses of pseudoprofessionalism would "be overcome by that humility which becomes the genuine scholar."[28] A true humility might well be out of style, but it remained an enduring ideal for the "perfect" historian.

Many historians concluded in the postwar period that integrity was also most important for historians. Having seen the vicious uses to which history had been put by dictator and democrat alike, the historian had a strong feeling that the qualities of justice, impartiality, and objectivity were the only ones that could protect him from future enslavement as a propagandist and allow him to perform those critical functions so necessary to a world in which all words had become suspect. Most of these sentiments can be summarized in two sentences of Hans Schmitt about the historian: "He should be a man of principle. He should strive to assemble impartially as much evidence as he can and then attempt to interpret it in accord with the dictates of a sensitive conscience."[29]

Those qualities which postwar historians in looking at themselves decided were the ideal ones constituted a blending of the traditional with the innovative. But their configuration represented a fresh and dynamic concept of what the historian should be. It was a concept especially geared to the contemporary crisis and one which

[28] Wayne S. Cole, "American Entry into World War II: An Historiographical Appraisal," *Mississippi Valley Historical Review*, Vol. XLIII (March, 1957), 617; J. G. Randall, "Historianship," *American Historical Review*, Vol. LVIII (January, 1953), 253.

[29] Hans A. Schmitt, "Perspective: A Note on Historical Judgments," *South Atlantic Quarterly*, Vol. LXII (Winter, 1963), 62. Other useful statements defining historical integrity are W. Henry Cooke, "History and International Misunderstanding," *Pacific Historical Review*, Vol. XV (September, 1946), 305–11; Savelle, "Historian's Progress, or, The Quest for Sancta Sophia," *Pacific Historical Review*, Vol. XXVII (February, 1958), 11–12; Roy F. Nichols, "Adaptation Versus Invention as Elements in Historical Analysis," American Philosophical Society *Proceedings*, Vol. CVIII (October 20, 1964), 404.

sought to unite the scholar and the man into an instrument capable of speaking with both authority and sympathy to his fellow men. By emphasizing those traits often rejected in the past by advocates of scientific history yet retaining many of the qualities long connected with objective history, reflective historians were essaying a difficult passage between the Scylla of science and the Charybdis of passion. No one could expect all historians to embody all the qualities suggested. That would produce the perfect historian, and he was likely to remain a useful myth. But in a conscious striving toward those ideals lay hope that the passage could be attained without shipwreck.

The postwar introspection undertaken by historians brought to the surface of historiographical thought a fresh analysis of that oldest of questions: What is history? It was a question which had been debated, contemplated, and argued from the first time man attempted to preserve in some coherent fashion his memory of the past. Each generation, each period in time, had formulated its own particular definition, and the substance of those definitions had, in their own way, said as much about the times in which they had been constructed as they did about history. It was to be no different for contemporary writers. They too reflected the world in which they found themselves. Since that world was one afflicted with accelerating change, great confusion, and a debilitating uncertainty, it could be expected that definitions of history would mirror those conditions. It was not to be hoped that any kind of final or complete definition would be reached. But the very tentativeness of the gropings of historians for a new understanding of their subject demonstrated a willingness to face realistically the doubts and frustrations of the present age.

The matter of deciding upon a proper definition for history was confounded for American historians by the fact that the assault upon the premises of scientific history initiated by relativist thinkers like Carl Becker and Charles Beard had never been fully digested or accommodated. The shock of war and its demands had followed too closely upon the intramural squabbling of the late twenties and thirties for any reasonable compromise or *modus vivendi* to become operative. The sorting out of ideas, the acceptance or rejection of certain themes, and the clarification of premise and hypothesis so essential to rational thought largely had to wait for the period after

131

1945. It was then done in more or less piecemeal fashion; no organized or formal theory was enunciated. But there did occur a re-evaluation and reorientation which for the first time tried to incorporate the relativist critique into the main dimensions of American historical thought.

Primary among the achievements of the relativists had been that of clarifying the distinction between history and written history which had been considerably blurred during the heyday of the scientific school. There never really had been any quarrel except among some of the more esoteric philosophers about the existence of a historical past. The individual's own personal experience, as well as the material remains of yesterday, confirmed and validated that existence. Few would complain of a definition of this history as the record of all that man had done or thought in the past. What was in question was the accessibility of that true and agreed-upon past. To what degree was it reclaimable by the historian? And when presented in the form of written history, how well did it conform to the real past?

Underlying most of the assumptions of the scientific historians was the belief that through the application of the scientific method, adopted largely from the natural and physical sciences, a true picture —almost a photograph—of past reality could be obtained. There was an almost arrogant confidence in the ability of the method to accomplish this as if it were possible to divorce the instrument from its operator.[1] The more sure the historian became in the reliability of his technique, the more confident he became that the written history he produced was indeed the past reality everyone knew was there. As late as 1963, Milton Gold could lament the deterioration in historical writing, which he attributed to the pervasive influence of scientific historiography.[2] Yet the relativist attack on this major presupposition of the scientific school was basically successful in that the wide chasm between history and written history was again clearly

---

[1] See the comments of Theodore Maynard, "Muse and the Myth," *Catholic World*, Vol. CLXXXIII (July, 1956), 270–75.

[2] Milton Gold, "In Search of a Historian," *Centennial Review*, Vol. VII (Summer, 1963), 304–305.

demonstrated. If the extreme statement by Charles Beard that "written history was an act of faith" was not completely accepted, it was nevertheless true that historians were again compelled to recognize that the two histories were by no means identical. From that starting point came the new evaluation.

In contradicting the pretensions of scientific history the relativists also challenged a concept much older than the nineteenth century: the idea that from history there could be distilled as early Chinese culture had maintained, "a universal, timeless, abstract morality."[3] This idea had also been implicit in much of Graeco-Roman and Christian historiography, as well as that of the Enlightenment. While the relativists still proclaimed the utility of history, it was a pragmatic variety conditioned to whatever contemporary usage needs might dictate. Certainly, the notions of universality, timelessness, and abstract morality were not part of the relativist definition. Relativism, then, was much more than an attack upon the claim of the scientific historian to objectivity; it was additionally a rejection of the idea that anything of permanent value could be gained from historical study. "Why history," said Beard, "is just a cat dragged by its tail to places it rarely wants to go. Another man with a different social view could have used the same materials and written a volume with the opposite effect."[4] Even the relativist thinkers did not permit the logic of their position to stop them from writing and studying history, but the logic was nevertheless implicit in their affirmations. Taken to the extreme, it argued the futility of historical study.

Historians were never quite as comfortable after the relativist critique as they had been before. Even those who were prone to ignore the philosophical implications inherent in the study of history were forced to agree to the more telling points of the relativist rationale. By the end of World War II crucial segments of the relativist dogma had been admitted into the canons of the profession and had almost become clichés. One can discover statement after state-

3 Joseph R. Levenson, "Redefinition of Ideas in Time: The Chinese Classics and History," *Far Eastern Quarterly*, Vol. XV (May, 1956), 401.

4 Quoted in Eric F. Goldman, "The Origins of Beard's *Economic Interpretation of the Constitution*," *Journal of the History of Ideas*, Vol. XIII (April, 1952), 249.

ment attesting to this fact. As representative as any was contained in the beginning of the book by Ray Billington and others examining national bias in Anglo-American history textbooks:

> No matter how dedicated the historian is to the unembroidered truth, that truth is forever beyond his grasp, for no two students can ever view the past through the same eyes, or speak of what they see with the same lips. Each individual subconsciously reveals his own beliefs and prejudices in every line that he writes. . . . The historian views and records events relative to the time and place in which he lives.[5]

William O. Aydelotte confessed that the bias of the historian can be cultural as well as personal and that, although there was the possibility that through self-analysis and the criticism of his colleagues he might escape the former, there was little chance that he could free himself from the latter.[6] Yet, despite their general acceptance of major parts of the relativist hypothesis, few were willing to abandon two milleniums of historiographical tradition and assert the complete lack of validity in historical research and study. The demands also placed upon the profession by the world crisis with its hunger for some kind of certainty has led to a modification of the relativist position and a rather diffused attempt to forge a definition of history which retains the openness of relativism while rejecting its capacity for cynicism.

Avenues of reappraisal were opened with the recognition that there were at least two serious defects in the relativist chain of ideas. The first concerned the postulate that historical knowledge was unverifiable or unknowable in the strictest scientific sense. The idea that historians could never be sure of their data because of the subjective element of the historian worried Roy F. Nichols as early as 1948. To espouse a doctrine of uncertainty could vitiate all

[5] Ray Allen Billington *et al.*, *The Historian's Contribution to Anglo-American Misunderstanding*, 2. Other excellent statements are Wallace K. Ferguson, review of G. R. Potter (ed.), *The New Cambridge Modern History*, Vol. I, *The Renaissance, 1493–1520*, in *American Historical Review*, Vol. LXIII (April, 1958), 649; and Leo Gershoy, "Some Problems of a Working Historian," in Hook (ed.), *Philosophy and History: A Symposium*, 67.

[6] Aydelotte, "Notes on Historical Generalization," in Gottschalk (ed.), *Generalization in the Writing of History*, 158.

confidence and allow the most pernicious of habits to control research and writing. At best such a frame of reference could produce a lethargy fatal to continuing historical labor. A powerful article by Chester M. Destler in 1950 addressed itself to this particular problem. Destler, drawing heavily from the philosophical work of Maurice Mandelbaum and Arthur Lovejoy, stoutly maintained the reality and integrity of the historical past and the ability of the historian to comprehend it. He argued that the empirical nature of historical data was undeniable inasmuch as it was composed of physical remains—documents, archaeological finds, and the like. To Destler the crucial point for the historian was the ability to interpret the relationships among the phenomena of an earlier age. He felt confident that this interpretation was possible since psychologists believed that "a characteristic trait of the human mind is the ability to recognize relationships between data."[7] While Destler did not attack the merits of all relativist claims, he did demonstrate forcefully that there was another side to the argument concerning the validity of historical data.

Writing also in 1950, Lewis Beck, viewing from the vantage point of philosophy rather than history, pointed to what he believed was "the Achilles heel of relativism." Beck declared that the skepticism of relativist thought was essentially inconsistent in that the relativist found it impossible to be skeptical about his own skepticism. "He tries to be skeptical of all histories, but he cannot be skeptical of histories of histories. He will insist endlessly on the impossibility of understanding the Roman Empire, but he will claim without hesitation an understanding of the personality and biases of Edward Gibbon, Theodor Mommsen, and everyone else who has written on the subject."[8] Beck was illustrating the applicability of the

<hr/>

[7] Roy F. Nichols, "Postwar Reorientation of Historical Thinking," *American Historical Review*, Vol. LIV (October, 1948), 79; Chester M. Destler, "Some Observations on Contemporary Historical Theory," *American Historical Review*, Vol. LV (April, 1950), 516. Destler's article also contains a convenient summary of the relativist faith. See p. 507.

[8] Lewis W. Beck, "The Limits of Skepticism in History," *South Atlantic Quarterly*, Vol. XLIX (October, 1950), 462–63. See also Edward Pessen, "Can Historians Be Objective?" *Bulletin* of the Association of American Colleges, Vol. XLI (May,

old philosophy-class "stopper": If all statements are relative, then so is this one. Regardless of its simplicity, however, Beck's criticism was pertinent. There were indeed limits to skepticism, and the relativist's paradox of not being skeptical about his own skepticism dramatically delineated those limits. The redefinition of history attempted by postwar historians gained much from these two intellectual chinks in the relativist armor.

Despite the postwar questioning of the ultimate implications of relativist historiography, historians relied heavily upon certain aspects of relativism for a reconstruction of the definition of history. The relativists had made too many telling points to be ignored completely. What occurred was that emphasis was given to particular relativist insights that seemed especially meaningful and relevant to the contemporary age. By far the most useful idea contributed by those who had attacked the schemata of scientific history was the avowal of the influence of the writing, practicing historian upon written history. The argument that history could never be totally objective because of the impact of the historian's personality and frame of reference was not only accepted generally at face value but also welcomed and expanded into a touchstone of the new definition. For just as historians had come to believe that a basic humanity was an essential ingredient in the makeup of the good historian, so they had also come to feel that good history was one which reflected the historian's humanity. Believing that the personal imprint of the writer of history was an inescapable determinant, the important thing to many historians came to be assurance that the influence would be a beneficent one. And that determination would be solely the result of what the historian himself set out to do, for, as Lee Benson tersely declared, "History is what historians do."[9]

Written history was thus the result of the interaction between the historian and his material. It "consists in the tensile relationship, within the historian's experience, between the raw material of

1955), 316–27; and Henry J. Marks, "Ground Under Our Feet: Beard's Relativism," *Journal of the History of Ideas*, Vol. XIV (October, 1953), 628–33.

9 Lee Benson, "On 'The Logic of Historical Narration,' " in Sidney Hook (ed.), *Philosophy and History*, 34.

humanity that comes to him from the outside and the concepts of intelligibility that he has developed within himself."[10] It is a meeting between the objective factors of his data and the subjective factors from himself. It would be unreasonable to expect the material once submitted to the inner workings of the historian's mind and personality to remain unchanged. In fact, no one would desire such a consequence. Unrefined history is as useless as any other unprocessed raw material. The finished product will bear the unmistakable stamp of the man who wrote it. If the writer is a superior craftsman and conscious of his aesthetic responsibility, what emerges is not just history but also a work of art and, like all art, something which has been fashioned by the temperament of the artist. "Zola once defined art as a piece of nature seen through a temperament; we may similarly define history as past events seen through a temperament."[11]

Historians have been insistent in projecting the image of historian as artist and in contrasting this notion with that equation of historian as photographer which seemed to typify the desired image of the scientific school. Harvey Wish said that "history is indeed an objective reality but not a photograph of the past," and Allan Nevins carried the metaphor further by flatly declaring that "the idea that history is photography is set at naught." Calling for the continual rewriting of history, Nevins believed that history "constantly requires a new mixture of pigments, new points of view, new manipulation of light and shade." Of course, the quality of the completed picture depends upon the skilled technique of the painter and the caliber of his sensitivity. "After all," said Arthur M. Schlesinger, Jr., "written history is the application of an aesthetic vision to a welter of facts; and both the weight and vitality of a historical work depend on the quality of the vision."[12]

10 Leonard Krieger, review of Henri-Irénée Marrow, *De La Connaissance Historique*, in *American Historical Review*, Vol. LXIV (January, 1959), 332.

11 Hans Kohn, "A Historian's Creed for Our Time," *South Atlantic Quarterly*, Vol. LII (July, 1953), 348; Felix Reichmann, "Historical Research and Library Science," *Library Trends*, Vol. XIII (July, 1964), 33.

12 Harvey Wish, "The American Historian and the New Conservatism," *South Atlantic Quarterly*, Vol. LXV (Spring, 1966), 191; Allan Nevins, "Should American

But the historical writer, like the graphic artist, must always keep in mind his audience. What he hopes to do is to evoke from his readers a measured response to his artistic endeavors—to get them to view a certain thing in a way similar to his own. If he can accomplish this, his art has been successful. Crane Brinton earlier said it very well: "The writing of history is, like the preaching of a sermon, an art, and its success is to be measured less by its conformity with rules established by the critics than by its effect on its audience." The vision of the historian is always truth as he perceives the raw materials through the filter of his own personality. Through his history he tries to share this truth—to make it a part of remembered experience for everyone. No matter how disjointed and unconnected it all may seem to him at first perusal, he must somehow endow it with elements of pattern and unity which make it artistic, yet truthful. John D. Hicks confessed that "sometimes I wonder if history is not more like a series of unrelated explosions," but he also admitted that "I can never write it that way." No historian can, because "history is an imaginative reconstruction of the past," which "while scientific in its methods and findings is artistic in its presentation."[13]

In deploring the loss of the great prose stylists of the nineteenth century in the writing of history, Russel B. Nye put his finger on the principal reason for lament. By eschewing vivid rhetoric as too romantic and by hiding the personality of the writer behind a bland style, historians had lost that humanity which emerges only when the reader is made aware of the impact of the historian's personality on his material.[14] A denial of style was in essence a denial of personality, a dehumanization which transformed what should be alive and vibrant into a bloodless recital without sparkle, wit, or life.

History Be Rewritten?" in Eisenstadt (ed.), *The Craft of American History*, I, 179; Schlesinger, "The Historian as Artist," *Atlantic*, Vol. CCXIII (July, 1963), 36.

[13] Crane Brinton, "The New History: Twenty-Five Years After," *Journal of Social Philosophy*, Vol. I (January, 1936), 142; John D. Hicks, "The Personal Factor in the Writing of History," *Pacific Northwest Quarterly*, Vol. LV (July, 1964), 103; Mark M. Krug, "History and the Social Sciences," *Social Education*, Vol. XXIX (December, 1965), 515.

[14] Russel B. Nye, *George Bancroft: Brahmin Rebel*, 285.

Rather than work toward a removal from history of the writer's imprint, historians should endeavor to make that imprint indelible and unmistakable. Whether it was in the classroom or on the printed page, historians had a responsibility to their audience who would remember a point of view "long after they have forgotten the facts we communicated to them."[15] The historian could not separate himself from his history; nor should he wish to do so. For only in openly admitting the relationship and overtly exploiting it could his artistry be enhanced and his influence be increased. "History," affirmed Philip D. Jordan, "should be an adventure of the mind;"[16] it had great affinity with literature and the fine arts. An important part of any definition of history and perhaps its starting point in addition, was the candid statement that the historian and the history he wrote were intertwined and inseparable.

History defined as an artistic re-creation of past life, while a useful beginning, did not go far enough. It needed to be elaborated and explained. Other things as well as history could be included in such a definition. There had to be unique qualities which differentiated history from some of its cohorts. The novel, for example, could also be construed frequently as an artistic recreation of past life. Even a single painting might well be allowed under the protective shade of such a wide umbrella. What did history possess that set it apart? What gave it a special identity? What made it history?

One of its distinguishing characteristics was its preservation of the uniqueness of past experience and its resultant preoccupation with the processes of change. History was never a twice-told tale but rather the presentation of singular people and events within the conformity of human nature. Similarities might be noted and comparisons duly made, but all historical periods and all historical events had a flavor, a pungency all their own. It might well be argued, as James C. Malin contended, that the worth of written history "is to be found in the degree to which it preserves that uniqueness in

[15] Perkins, "We Shall Gladly Teach," *American Historical Review*, Vol. LXII (January, 1957), 299.
[16] Philip D. Jordan, "The Usefulness of Useless Knowledge," *Historian*, Vol. XXII (May, 1960), 240– 41.

manageable form."[17] History obviously can be made more effective if the historian is adept in the technique of comparison and contrast, in the drawing of revealing analogies, and in the employment of modern terminology, but the reader must come away from his reading having been supplied the particular, never-to-be-repeated atmosphere of the period under study. The French Revolution was distinct and unique. The activities of Lenin in 1917 may well illuminate the work of Robespierre in 1793; however, Lenin and Robespierre were not identical. The historian contends not that *every* fact is unique but that every combination of facts produces something entirely different from any preceding or succeeding combination.[18] Preoccupation with uniqueness must be added to any definition of history.

Another aspect of the nature of history is its relation to memory. As has been noted earlier, one of the major functions of history is to act as the collective memory of mankind. In fact, this was probably its earliest task. But the historical memory is a special kind of memory which differs significantly from the memory that is put to use by every individual in his navigation of everyday life. Its primary variable is its structuring and order. Whereas individual memory relies on a storehouse of often unrelated data, some important and some trivial, historical memory has been refined by the historian into convenient and, it is hoped, useful compartments. Additionally, historical memory is painfully self-conscious and the result of deliberate reflection.[19] It constantly informs mankind about where he has been and performs the task of forever reminding him of his predilections for both good and evil.

It is the act of reflection which distinguishes the historical memory from the work of the chronicler or the individual's use of memory as tool. "The examined memory of the past is history in the highest and fullest sense." While ordinary memory is uncritical, historical mem-

---

17 J. C. Malin, *The Contriving Brain and the Skillful Hand in the United States: Something About History and Philosophy of History*, 339.

18 Stanley Pargellis, "Clio in a Strait Jacket," *American Quarterly*, Vol. XI (Summer, 1959), 230.

19 Bertram D. Wolfe, "Operation Rewrite: The Agony of Soviet Historians," *Foreign Affairs*, Vol. XXXI (October, 1952), 57.

ory represents a process in which the historian has confronted mountains of raw data and has reflected upon their meanings. He has thought about his evidence; history is not just a bald recounting of past events or time or people; it is putting it together and coming to some conclusions about what it all meant. The historian brings to that task all the implements available to him in the present age, and consequently "history is not the mere memory of humanity but the reformation of its memory."[20] Any definition of history which has any pretensions to accuracy must reflect the idea of examined memory. But history is also more than this: it is itself part of a continuing process, a perpetual becoming. And it is this ongoing fluidity which has seemed particularly entrancing to postwar historians and constitutes their chief contribution to redefinition.

Historical analysts have come to recognize since 1945 the continuum character of both actual history and the written history which tries to duplicate it. Partly the result of evolutionary doctrine and partly the product of a reading of the times, historical thought has begun to ponder the implications of its discovery for the profession. The full import of the revelation has not yet been felt; only a few have dealt with the problem. But enough has been written to suggest the general outlines which the investigation so far has taken and to adumbrate what lines are likely to be pursued in the future.

Refinements of evolutionary theory had already made it clear to historians that the actuality of the historical process was not one which could be circumscribed by arbitrary beginnings and endings. Reality was distorted when the historian, acting the role of surgeon, made a precise incision at 1066 and extracted everything up to 1120. History was not something which could be so neatly excised, because part of the vitality of history, that which gave it its dynamism, was an ongoing process. Nothing was ever static; things were always moving. Any particular moment in historical time contained elements of the past in its present, as well as the growth seeds of the future.

[20] Cantor, *Medieval History*, 3; Perez Zagorin, "Carl Becker on History," *American Historical Review*, Vol. LXII (October, 1956), 9; Leonard Krieger, "Horizons of History," *American Historical Review*, Vol. LXIII (October, 1957), 73.

Darwin and his followers had demonstrated beyond question the movement inherent in the developmental process, and there was no reason to believe that history was in any way immune from its operation. J. H. Hexter caught the feeling well: "For history is a becoming, an ongoing, and it is to be understood not only in terms of what comes before but also of what comes after."[21]

Historians did not really need the example of Darwin to convince them of the validity of a hypothesis which stated the idea of dynamic growth. The personal experience of any historian begins, as it does for all persons, with the historical present. A logical extrapolation of that present leads backward to a series of historical presents—each moving, each merging into a succeeding present, each flowing onto the present. One can find in almost any great historian a fondness for the river metaphor: the likening of history, or time, to that of a stream following an often tortuous route to the sea. This idea is very close to the evolutionary idea of ongoing change and development. But certainly the acceptance by the natural sciences of Darwinism effectively buttressed the historian's conventional viewpoint. Additionally, since change has always been a major preoccupation of historians, it was only natural that they should tend to focus on the inner workings of the process itself. In fact, historians determine that "an action becomes historical when it is viewed as the intermediate point of a temporal process in which it is produced, and then in turn helps to produce a subsequent action."[22] Historians are likely to pass over the history of a society which remains static for any length of time, when change is imperceptible; the history of paleolithic man would probably be very dull were it available. It is the unfolding of events over time and space which are interesting and which have convinced historians that history is an unfolding and the historian not an outside observer but, himself, a part of the becoming.[23]

21 Hexter, *Reappraisals in History*, 11–12.

22 Leonard Krieger, "Comments on Historical Explanation," in Sidney Hook (ed.), *Philosophy and History: A Symposium*, 140–41.

23 Statements concerning the notion of the fluid character of history may be found in Robert E. Brown, "Liberalism, Conservatism, and History," *Centennial Review*, Vol. VII (Summer, 1963), 323; James C. Bonner, "The Writing of History,"

The accelerating rate of change which has accompanied the twentieth century has likewise been responsible for reaffirming the historian's belief in the omnipresence of movement. True, change has often been so rapid and so far-reaching that understanding seems impossible, and it has made the task of the historian ever more formidable. For a while mankind appeared to be moving slowly down the river of time, periodically even becalmed; however, the recent pace has been so furious and the rapids so many that the boat seems sure to capsize. The historian since World War II has been made increasingly aware that he is a passenger on the boat and not a disinterested observer ashore, amused and entertained by the spectacle.

Written history, as well as actual history, is also a continuing process. What was taken as historical truth yesterday may be revised and modified tomorrow. New records come to light, new techniques are devised, new insights are obtained. Because of its tentative nature it can never be complete. This is one characteristic which history shares with science. It is "a discipline capable of progress as well as regression."[24] The same periods, people, and events of history are constantly re-examined; new questions are asked of old data. Actually, historians have attacked history piecemeal, that is, delineating a single age or occurrence for study and dissection. Sidney Mead avowed that "every written history is essentially an assertion in the form of a thesis that constitutes an answer to a question about the past." The one thing any historian can be sure of is that some future historian will refute or change what he has written. But there was hope that written history was not simply an exercise in futility, an absorbing pastime of ephemeral value. Charles G. Sellers taught that the accumulation of historical knowledge, however zigzag the course, "brings us ever closer vantage points for discerning its [objective reality's] salient features." The fact that written history too was a continuing mechanism did not obviate its worth as an illuminant

Georgia Review, Vol. XIV (Fall, 1960), 337; and Lee Benson, "Research Problems in American Political Historiography," in Mirra Komarovsky (ed.), *Common Frontiers of the Social Sciences*, 116.

24 Peter Gay, *A Loss of Mastery: Puritan Historians in Colonial America*, 122.

or denigrate its significance. In Arthur Bestor's words, "History is that sufficient image of the past which each generation formulates to make intelligible the world about it." Whatever history did, said Wendell Stephenson, it "should be synonymous with understanding."[25]

Historians and their reading public must content themselves, then, with the realization that in history there are no final victories.[26] Perhaps the most important part of any definition of history is that which acknowledges this fact. One can never be absolutely certain about the history he reads or writes. He must be satisfied with Bestor's "sufficient image." And that image will vary from individual to individual and from generation to generation. The conclusion of Henry Adams that all historical interpretation is relative and all understanding is tentative was sufficient and useful to him. "It made sense of what . . . was otherwise chaos."[27] The historian who expects more expects too much, and it will not be forthcoming. The experience is frustrating, and many will, at given times, share some pessimistic thoughts with Garrett Mattingly:

> I do not think it is really quite as bad as that, but in my more pessimistic moments I am sometimes inclined to imagine that the historical profession, instead of moving steadily through experience and self-criticism to deeper understanding and steadier, more penetrating vision, just swings aimlessly back and forth with the tides of fashion, like the ladies' garment industry.[28]

But the conscious acceptance of both the professional and the personal limitations imposed by the study of history can also act as a positive aid. Unfinished history, unfolding history, leaves room

[25] Mead, "Church History Explained," *Church History*, Vol. XXXII (March, 1963), 19; Charles G. Sellers, "Andrew Jackson Versus the Historians," 634; Arthur Bestor, "The Humaneness of History," in Eisenstadt (ed.), *The Craft of American History*, I, 5; Wendell H. Stephenson, "A Quarter Century of American Historiography," *Mississippi Valley Historical Review*, Vol. XLV (June, 1958), 21–22.

[26] Smith, *The Historian and History*, 198.

[27] John C. Cairns, "The Successful Quest of Henry Adams," *South Atlantic Quarterly*, Vol. LVII (Spring, 1958), 192–93.

[28] Garrett Mattingly, "Some Revisions of the Political History of the Renaissance," in Tinsely Hilton (ed.), *The Renaissance*, 9.

in which the role of the historian, and his audience, can be formative, a perpetual challenge to ingenuity and honesty.

Finally, in attempting a redefinition of history, postwar historians have at last begun to accept history as something which cannot be defined by comparing and contrasting it with other disciplines. For too long historians have been arguing whether history was art or science, whether it was humanity or social science. Sometimes envious of the prestige of the physical sciences, sometimes jealous of the artistic freedom of the fine arts, historians have frequently sought refuge in one or the other camp. It is to be hoped that that debate has ended with the knowledge that history is its own master, with its own methods, artistry, and reason for being.[29] It need not apologize or feel inferior or justify its existence. History is history. In accepting its uniqueness and in welcoming its challenges, historians can contribute much to a world which desperately needs to understand itself. The pursuit of history despite its frustrations and insecurities continues to be a noble and exciting venture.

[29] See comments by Roy F. Nichols, "Postwar Reorientation of Historical Thinking," 84; Woodward, *The Burden of Southern History*, 38–39; Stanley Pargellis, "Clio in a Strait Jacket," *American Quarterly*, Vol. XI (Summer, 1959), 231.

Bibliography

The following list represents a selection of those books and articles which were most useful for this study. No attempt has been made to compile a list which would include everything consulted in the process of research. It is hoped that the bibliography will guide the reader who is interested in exploring further the rich and varied literature available.

BOOKS

Adcock, F. E. *Thucydides and His History.* New York, Cambridge University Press, 1963.

Altick, Richard D. *The Scholar Adventurers.* New York, Macmillan Co., 1951.

Anscombe, G. E. M. "Reality of the Past," in Max Black, ed., *Philosophical Analysis.* Ithaca, Cornell University Press, 1950.

Arendt, Hannah. *Between Past and Future.* New York, Viking Press, 1961.

———. *The Human Condition.* Chicago, University of Chicago Press, 1958.

———. *The Origins of Totalitarianism.* New York, Harcourt, Brace, and Co., 1951.

Aron, Raymond. *The Century of Total War.* Garden City, Doubleday and Co., 1954.

———. *Introduction to the Philosophy of History: An Essay on the Limits of Historical Objectivity.* Trans. by George J. Irwin. Boston, Beacon Press, 1961.

Ausubel, Herman. *Historians and Their Craft: A Study of the Presidential Addresses to the American Historical Association, 1884–1945.* New York, Columbia University Press, 1952.

———, J. B. Brebner, and E. M. Hunt (eds.). *Some Modern Historians of Britain.* New York, Dryden Press, 1951.

Barnes, Harry E. *Historical Sociology: Its Origins and Development: Theories of Social Evolution, from Cave Life to Atomic Bombing.* New York, Philosophical Library, 1948.

———. *A History of Historical Writing.* 2d rev. ed. New York, Dover Publishers, Inc., 1962.

Barzun, Jacques. *Darwin, Marx, and Wagner.* 2d ed. New York, Doubleday and Co., 1957.

———, and H. F. Graff. *The Modern Researcher.* New York, Harcourt, Brace and Co., 1957.

Baxter, Maurice G., Robert H. Ferrell, and John E. Wiltz. *The Teaching of American History in High Schools.* Bloomington, Indiana University Press, 1964.

Bailey, Thomas A. *Woodrow Wilson and the Great Betrayal.* New York, Quadrangle Books, Inc., 1963.

———. *Woodrow Wilson and the Lost Peace.* New York, Quadrangle Books, Inc., 1963.

Beale, Howard K. *Charles A. Beard: An Appraisal.* Lexington, University of Kentucky Press, 1954.

———. *Theodore Roosevelt and the Rise of America to World Power.* New York, P. F. Collier, Inc., 1962.

Bellot, H. Hale. *American History and American Historians.* Norman, University of Oklahoma Press, 1952.

Bendix, Reinhard. *Max Weber: An Intellectual Portrait.* Garden City Doubleday and Co., 1960.

Berelson, Bernard, *et al. The Social Studies and the Social Sciences.* New York, Harcourt, Brace, and World, 1962.

Berlin, Isaiah. *The Hedgehog and the Fox.* New York, Mentor Books, 1957.

———. *Historical Inevitability.* London, Oxford University Press, 1954.

Berman, Milton. *John Fiske: The Evolution of a Popularizer.* Harvard Historical Monographs, no. 48. Cambridge, Harvard University Press, 1961.

Benson, Lee. *Turner and Beard: American Historical Writing Reconsidered.* Glencoe, Illinois, Free Press, 1960.

Billington, Ray A., C. P. Hill, *et al. The Historian's Contribution to Anglo-American Misunderstanding: Report of a Committee on National Bias in Anglo-American History Textbooks.* New York, Hobbs, Dorman and Co., 1966.

———, ed. *The Reinterpretation of Early American History: Essays in*

Honor of John E. Pomfret. San Marino, California, Huntington Library, 1966.

Bloch, Marc. *The Historian's Craft.* New York, Alfred A. Knopf Co., 1953.

Borning, Bernard C. *The Political and Social Thought of Charles A. Beard.* Seattle, University of Washington Press, 1962.

Bowen, Catherine Drinker. *Adventures of a Biographer.* Boston, Atlantic, Little, Brown, and Co., 1959.

Bremner, Robert H., ed. *Essays on History and Literature.* Columbus, Ohio State University Press, 1966.

Brumfitt, J. H. *Voltaire, Historian.* New York, Oxford University Press, 1958.

Bunge, Mario. *Causality: The Place of the Causal Principle in Modern Science.* Cambridge, Harvard University Press, 1959.

Bury, J. B. *Selected Essays.* Ed. by H. Temperley. Chicago, Argonaut, Inc., Publishers, 1967.

Butterfield, Herbert. *History and Human Relations.* London, Collins, Inc., 1951.

———. *Man on His Past: The Study of the History of Historical Scholarship.* Boston, Beacon Press, 1960.

———. *The Whig Interpretation of History.* London, G. Bell and Sons, 1931.

Cantor, Norman E. *Medieval History.* New York, Macmillan Co., 1963.

———, and Richard I. Schneider. *How to Study History.* New York, Thomas Y. Crowell Co., 1967.

Carr, Edward Hallett. *What Is History?* New York, Alfred A. Knopf, Inc., 1962.

Caughey, J. W. *Hubert Howe Bancroft: Historian of the West.* Berkeley, University of California Press, 1946.

Childe, V. Gordon. *What Is History?* New York, H. Schuman, 1953.

Clagett, Marshall, ed. *Critical Problems in the History of Science.* Madison, University of Wisconsin Press, 1959.

Clough, Shepard. *The Rise and Fall of Civilizations: An Inquiry into the Relationship Between Economic Development and Civilization.* New York, McGraw-Hill, 1951.

Cohen, Warren I. *The American Revisionists: The Lessons of Intervention in World War I.* Chicago, University of Chicago Press, 1967.

Cohnman, Werner J., and Alvin Boskoff, eds. *Sociology and History: Theory and Research.* New York, Free Press of Glencoe, 1964.

Colbourn, H. Trevor. *The Lamp of Experience: Whig History and the Intellectual Origins of the American Revolution.* Chapel Hill, University of North Carolina Press, 1965.

Collingwood, R. G. *The Idea of History.* New York, Oxford University Press, 1957.

Commager, Henry S. *The Search for a Usable Past and Other Essays in Historiography.* New York, Alfred A. Knopf, Inc., 1967.

Cooke, Jacob E. *Frederic Bancroft: Historian.* Norman, University of Oklahoma Press, 1957.

Coulborn, Rushton, ed. *Feudalism in History.* Princeton, Princeton University Press, 1956.

———. *The Origin of Civilized Societies.* Princeton, Princeton University Press, 1959.

Crocker, Lester G. *An Age of Crisis: Man and the World in Eighteenth Century French Thought.* Baltimore, Johns Hopkins Press, 1959.

Cruden, Robert. *James Ford Rhodes: The Man, the Historian, and His Work.* Cleveland, Press of Western Reserve University, 1961.

Curti, Merle. *Probing Our Past.* New York, Harper & Brothers, 1955.

———, ed. *American Scholarship in the Twentieth Century.* Cambridge, Harvard University Press, 1953.

Danto, Arthur C. *Analytical Philosophy of History.* New York, Cambridge University Press, 1965.

Denton, Robert C., ed. *The Idea of History in the Ancient Near East.* New Haven, Yale University Press, 1955.

Donovan, Timothy Paul. *Henry Adams and Brooks Adams: The Education of Two American Historians.* Norman, University of Oklahoma Press, 1961.

Doughty, Howard. *Francis Parkman.* New York, Macmillan Co., 1962.

Dovring, Folke. *History as a Social Science: An Essay on the Nature and Purpose of Historical Studies.* The Hague, Martinus Nijhoff, 1960.

Eisenstadt, A. S. *Charles McLean Andrews: A Study in American Historical Writing.* New York, Columbia University Press, 1955.

———, ed. *The Craft of American History.* 2 vols. New York, Harper & Row, 1966.

Emerson, Donald E. *Richard Hildreth.* Baltimore, Johns Hopkins Press, 1946.

Engle, Shirley H., ed. *New Perspectives in World History.* Thirty-Fourth Yearbook of the National Council for the Social Studies. Washington, D.C., The Council, 1964.

Engel-Janosi, Friedrich. *Four Studies in French Romantic Historical Writing*. Baltimore, Johns Hopkins Press, 1955.

Feis, Herbert, *et al. The Historian and the Diplomat: The Role of History and Historians in American Foreign Policy*. Ed. by Francis L. Loewenheim. New York, Harper & Row, 1967.

Ferguson, Wallace K. *The Renaissance in Historical Thought: Five Centuries of Interpretation*. Boston, Houghton Mifflin Co., 1948.

Finberg, H. P. R., ed. *Approaches to History: A Symposium*. Toronto, University of Toronto Press, 1962.

Fisher, Ruth Anna, and William L. Fox. *J. Franklin Jameson: A Tribute*. Washington, D.C., Catholic University of America Press, 1965.

Fitzsimons, Mathew A., Alfred G. Pundt, and Charles E. Nowell, eds. *The Development of Historiography*. Harrisburg, Stackpole Co., 1955.

Flower, Milton E. *James Parton: The Father of Modern Biography*. Durham, Duke University Press, 1951.

Furber, Elizabeth C., ed. *Changing Views on British History: Essays on Historical Writing Since 1939*. Cambridge, Harvard University Press, 1966.

Gardiner, C. Harvey, ed. *The Papers of William Hickling Prescott*. Urbana, University of Illinois Press, 1964.

Gardiner, Patrick, ed. *Theories of History: Readings from Classical and Contemporary Sources*. Glencoe, Free Press, 1959.

Gargan, Edward T., ed. *The Intent of Toynbee's History*. Chicago, Loyola University Press, 1961.

Garraghan, Gilbert J. and Jean Delanglez, eds. *A Guide to Historical Method*. New York, Fordham University Press, 1946.

Garraty, John A. *The Nature of Biography*. New York, Alfred A. Knopf, Inc., 1957.

Gatell, Frank O. *John Gorham Palfrey and the New England Conscience*. Cambridge, Harvard University Press, 1963.

Gay, Peter. *A Loss of Mastery: Puritan Historians in Colonial America*. Berkeley, University of California Press, 1966.

Geyl, Pieter. *Debates with Historians*. New York, Meridian Books, 1958.

———. *From Ranke to Toynbee: Five Lectures on Historians and Historiographical Problems*. Northampton, Smith College, 1952.

———. *Use and Abuse of History*. New Haven, Yale University Press, 1955.

———, P. Sorokin, and Arnold J. Toynbee. *The Pattern of the Past: Can We Determine It?* Boston, Beacon Press, 1949.

Ginsburg, Morris. *The Idea of Progress: A Revaluation.* Boston, Beacon Press, 1953.

Goldman, Eric F. "Fresh Winds in Historiography," in *Social Science Frontiers: Annual Proceedings of the Middle States: Council for the Social Studies,* 1951–52.

Gooch, G. P. *History and Historians in the Nineteenth Century.* Boston, Beacon Press, 1959.

Gottschalk, Louis. *Understanding History: A Primer of Historical Method.* New York, Alfred A. Knopf, Inc., 1950.

———, ed. *Generalization in the Writing of History: A Report of the Committee on Historical Analysis of the Social Science Research Council.* Chicago, University of Chicago Press, 1963.

———, Clyde Kluckhohn, and Robert Angell. "The Historian and the Historical Document," in *The Use of Personal Documents in History, Anthropology, and Sociology.* Social Science Research Council Bulletin 53. New York, 1945.

Gustavson, Carl A. *A Preface To History.* New York, McGraw-Hill Book Co., 1955.

Halperin, S. William, ed. *Some 20th Century Historians: Essays on Eminent Europeans.* Chicago, University of Chicago Press, 1961.

Hanke, Lewis. *Bartolomé de Las Casas: Historian.* Gainesville, University of Florida Press, 1952.

Harbison, E. Harris. *Christianity and History: Essays.* Princeton, Princeton University Press, 1964.

Helton, Tinsley, ed. *The Renaissance: A Reconsideration of the Theories and Interpretations of the Age.* Madison, University of Wisconsin Press, 1961.

Herbst, Jurgen. *The German Historical School in American Scholarship: A Study in the Transfer of Culture.* Ithaca, Cornell University Press, 1965.

Herr, Richard. *Tocqueville and the Old Regime.* Princeton, Princeton University Press, 1962.

Hexter, J. H. *Reappraisals in History.* Torchbook Edition. New York, Harper & Row, 1963.

Higham, John, *et al. History.* Englewood Cliffs, Prentice-Hall, Inc., 1965.

———, ed. *The Reconstruction of American History.* New York, Harper & Brothers, 1962.

Himmelfarb, Gertrude. *Lord Acton: A Study in Conscience and Politics.* Chicago, University of Chicago Press, 1952.

Hockett, Homer C. *The Critical Method in Historical Research and Writing.* New York, Macmillan Co., 1955.

Hook, Sidney. "Intelligence and Evil in Human History," in S. Hook and M. R. Konvitz, eds. *Freedom and Experience: Essays Presented to Horace M. Kallen.* New York, Cornell University Press, 1947.

————, ed. *Philosophy and History: A Symposium.* New York, New York University Press, 1963.

Hoselitz, Bert F., ed. *A Reader's Guide to the Social Sciences.* Glencoe, Free Press, 1959.

Hughes, H. Stuart. *Consciousness and Society, The Reorientation of European Social Thought.* Vintage Edition. New York, Alfred A. Knopf, Inc., 1961.

————. *An Essay of Our Times.* New York, Alfred A. Knopf, Inc., 1950.

————. *History as Art and as Science: Twin Vistas on the Past.* New York, Harper & Row, 1964.

————. *Oswald Spengler: A Critical Estimate.* New York, Charles Scribner's Sons, 1962.

————, ed. *Teachers of History: Essays in Honor of Lawrence B. Packard.* Ithaca, Cornell University Press, 1954.

Jelenski, K. A., ed. *History and Hope: Tradition, Ideology, and Change in Modern Society.* New York, Frederick A. Praeger Publishers, 1962.

Jordy, William. *Henry Adams: Scientific Historian.* New Haven, Yale University Press, 1952.

Kahler, Erich. *The Meaning of History.* New York, George Braziller, 1964.

Keyes, G. L. *Christian Faith and the Interpretation of History: A Study of St. Augustine's Philosophy of History.* Lincoln, University of Nebraska Press, 1966.

Knoles, George H., ed. *The Crisis of the Union, 1860–1861.* Baton Rouge, Louisiana State University Press, 1965.

Koenig, Duane, ed. *Historians and History: Essays in Honor of Charlton W. Tebeau.* Miami, University of Miami Press, 1966.

Komarovsky, Mirra, ed. *Common Frontiers of the Social Sciences.* Glencoe, Free Press, 1957.

Kraus, Michael. *The Writing of American History.* Norman, University of Oklahoma Press, 1953.

Krey, August C. *History and the Social Web: A Collection of Essays.* Minneapolis, University of Minnesota Press, 1955.

Kroeber, A. L. *The Nature of Culture*. Chicago, University of Chicago Press, 1952.

——. *Style and Civilizations*. Ithaca, Cornell University Press, 1957.

Laistner, M. L. W. *The Greater Roman Historians*. Berkeley, University of California Press, 1947.

Laquer, Walter, and George L. Mosse, eds. *The New History: Trends in Historical Research and Writing Since World War II*. New York, Harper & Row, 1966.

Levenson, J. C. *The Mind and Art of Henry Adams*. Boston, Houghton Mifflin Co., 1957.

Levin, David. *History as Romantic Art: Bancroft, Prescott, Motley, and Parkman*. Stanford, Stanford University Press, 1959.

Link, Arthur S., and Rembert W. Patrick, eds. *Writing Southern History: Essays in Historiography in Honor of Fletcher M. Green*. Baton Rouge, Louisiana State University Press, 1965.

Lord, Clifford L., ed. *Keepers of the Past*. Chapel Hill, University of North Carolina Press, 1965.

Lovejoy, Arthur O. *Essays in the History of Ideas*. Baltimore, Johns Hopkins Press, 1948.

Löwith, Karl. *Meaning in History*. Chicago, University of Chicago Press, 1949.

McIlwain, C. H. "The Historian," in R. B. Heywood, ed. *The Works of the Mind*. Chicago, University of Chicago Press, 1947.

McKeon, Richard. *Freedom and History: The Semantics of Philosophical Controversies and Ideological Conflicts*. New York, Noonday Press, 1952.

McNeill, William H. *Past and Future*. Chicago, University of Chicago Press, 1954.

——. *The Rise of the West: A History of the Human Community*. Chicago, University of Chicago Press, 1963.

Malin, J. C. *The Contriving Brain and the Skillful Hand in the United States: Something About History and Philosophy of History*. Lawrence, Kans., the author, 1955.

——. *Essays on Historiography*. Lawrence, Kans., the author, 1953.

——. *On the Nature of History: Essays about History and Dissidence*. Lawrence, Kan., the author, 1954.

Manuel, Frank E. *Shapes of Philosophical History*. Stanford, Stanford University Press, 1964.

Mazlish, Bruce. *The Riddle of History: The Great Speculators From Vico to Freud*. New York, Harper & Row, 1966.

Mason, Henry L. *Toynbee's Approach to World Politics*. New Orleans, Tulane University Press, 1958.

Mendell, Clarence W. *Tacitus: The Man and His Work*. New Haven, Yale University Press, 1957.

Meyerhoff, Hans, ed. *The Philosophy of History in Our Time*. Garden City, Doubleday, 1959.

Morison, Samuel Eliot. *By Land and By Sea: Essays and Addresses*. New York, Alfred A. Knopf, Inc., 1953.

————. *Vistas of History*. New York, Alfred A. Knopf, Inc., 1964.

Nef, John U. *War and Human Progress: An Essay on the Rise of Civilization*. Cambridge, Harvard University Press, 1950.

Neff, Emery. *The Poetry of History: The Contribution of Literature and Literary Scholarship to the Writing of History Since Voltaire*. New York, Columbia University Press, 1947.

Nevins, Allan. *The Gateway to History*. New York, Doubleday & Co., 1962.

Niebuhr, Reinhold. *Faith and History*. New York, Charles Scribner's Sons, 1949.

————. *The Irony of American History*. New York, Charles Scribner's Sons, 1952.

————. *The Self and the Dramas of History*. New York, Charles Scribner's Sons, 1955.

Noble, David W. *Historians Against History: The Frontier Thesis and the National Covenant in American Historical Writing Since 1830*. Minneapolis, University of Minnesota Press, 1965.

Nye, R. B. *George Bancroft: Brahmin Rebel*. New York, Alfred A. Knopf, Inc., 1945.

Parker, Harold T., and Richard Herr, eds. *Ideas in History: Essays Presented to Louis Gottschalk By His Former Students*. Durham, Duke University Press, 1965.

Pease, Otis A. *Parkman's History: The Historian as a Literary Artist*. New Haven, Yale University Press, 1953.

Perkins, Dexter, and John Snell. *The Education of Historians in the United States*. New York, McGraw-Hill Book Co., 1961.

Popper, Karl. *The Open Society and Its Enemies*. Rev. ed. Princeton, Princeton University Press, 1950.

————. *The Poverty of Historicism*. Boston, Beacon Press, 1957.

Quigley, Carroll. *The Evolution of Civilizations: An Introduction to Historical Analysis*. New York, Macmillan Co., 1961.

Randall, John H. *Nature and Historical Experience*. New York, Columbia University Press, 1958.

Rippy, J. Fred. *Bygones I Cannot Help Recalling: The Memoirs of a Mobile Scholar*. Austin, Steck-Vaughn Co., 1966.

Rockwood, Raymond O., ed. *Carl Becker's Heavenly City Revisited*. Ithaca, Cornell University Press, 1958.

Rotenstreich, Nathan. *Between Past and Present: An Essay on History*. New Haven, Yale University Press, 1958.

Samuels, Ernest. *Henry Adams: The Major Phase*. Cambridge, Harvard University Press, 1964.

————. *Henry Adams: The Middle Years*. Cambridge, Harvard University Press, 1958.

Sanders, Jennings. *Historical Interpretations and American Historianship*. Yellow Springs, Antioch Press, 1966.

Saveth, E. N., ed. *American History and the Social Sciences*. New York, Free Press, 1965.

Schevill, Ferdinand. *Six Historians*. Chicago, University of Chicago Press, 1956.

Schmitt, Bernadotte. *The Fashion and Future of History: Historical Studies and Addresses*. Cleveland, Western Reserve University Press, 1960.

Schoeck, Helmut, and J. W. Wiggins, eds. *Relativism and the Study of Man*. Princeton, D. Van Nostrand Co., 1961.

Schrecker, Paul. *Work and History: An Essay on the Structure of Civilization*. Princeton, Princeton University Press, 1948.

Skotheim, Allen. *American Intellectual Histories and Historians*. Princeton, Princeton University Press, 1966.

Smith, C. W. *Carl Becker: On History and the Climate of Opinion*. Ithaca, Cornell University Press, 1956.

Smith, Leslie F. *Modern Norwegian Historiography*. Oslo, Norwegian Universities Press, 1962.

Smith, Page. *The Historian and History*. New York, Alfred A. Knopf, Inc., 1964.

Smith, William R. *History as Argument: Three Patriot Historians of the American Revolution*. The Hague, Mouton & Co., 1966.

Social Science Research Council. *The Social Sciences in Historical Study:*

A Report of the Committee on Historiography. Bulletin 64. New York, 1954.

Stephenson, Wendell H. *Southern History in the Making: Pioneer Historians of the South.* Baton Rouge, Louisiana State University Press, 1964.

Stern, Fritz, ed. *Varieties of History.* New York, Meridian Books, 1956.

Strout, Cushing. *The Pragmatic Revolt in American History.* New Haven, Yale University Press, 1958.

Tholfsen, Trygve R. *Historical Thinking: An Introduction.* New York, Harper & Row, 1967.

Thompson, J. W. *History of Historical Writing.* 2 vols. New York, Macmillan Co., 1942.

Tindall, George B. *The Pursuit of Southern History: Presidential Addresses of the Southern Historical Association, 1935–1963.* Baton Rouge, Louisiana State University Press, 1964.

Van Tassel, David. *Recording America's Past: An Interpretation of the Development of Historical Studies in America, 1607–1884.* Chicago, University of Chicago Press, 1960.

Van Zandt, Roland. *The Metaphysical Foundations of American History.* The Hague, Mouton, & Co., 1959.

Voegelin, Eric. *Order and History.* 3 vols. Baton Rouge, Louisiana State University, 1956–57.

Von Laue, Theodore H. *Leopold Ranke: The Formative Years.* Princeton, Princeton University Press, 1950.

Webb, Walter P. *The Great Frontier.* Boston, Houghton Mifflin Co., 1952.

Weiss, Paul. *History: Written and Lived.* Carbondale, Southern Illinois University Press, 1962.

White, Leonard D., ed. *The State of the Social Sciences.* Chicago, University of Chicago Press, 1956.

White, Leslie A. *The Evolution of Culture.* New York, McGraw-Hill Book Co., 1959.

———. *The Science of Culture, a Study of Man and Civilization.* New York, Farrar, Straus, 1949.

White, Morton G. *Social Thought in America: The Revolt Against Formalism.* Boston, Beacon Press, 1957.

Wilkins, Burleigh Taylor. *Carl Becker.* Cambridge, Harvard University Press, 1961.

Wish, Harvey. *The American Historian: A Social-Intellectual History of the Writing of the American Past.* New York, Oxford University Press, 1960.

Woodward, C. Vann. *American Attitudes Toward History.* New York, Oxford University Press, 1955.

―――. *The Burden of Southern History.* New York, Vintage Books, 1961.

ARTICLES

Africa, Thomas W. "The City of God Revisited: Toynbee's Reconsiderations," *Journal of the History of Ideas,* Vol. XXIII (April–June, 1962), 282–92.

Alexander, Edward P. "New Faith in the American Heritage [historical societies in the United States]," *Maryland Historical Magazine,* Vol. LIV (March, 1959), 1–14.

Allen, Rodney F., and Joseph L. Fitzpatrick. "Using Poetry to Vitalize History," *Social Education,* Vol. XXIX (December, 1965), 529–31.

Anderson, Robert T. "Anthropology and History," *Bucknell Review,* Vol. XV (March, 1967), 1–8.

Arragon, R. F. "History's Changing Image: With Such Permanance as Time Has," *American Scholar,* Vol. XXXIII (Spring, 1964), 222–33.

Aydelotte, William O. "Quantification in History," *American Historical Review,* Vol. LXXI (April, 1966), 803–25.

Bailey, Thomas A. "America's Emergence as a World Power: The Myth and the Verity," *Pacific Historical Review,* Vol. XXX (February, 1961), 1–16.

Bainton, R. H. "Interpretations of the Reformation," *American Historical Review,* Vol. LXVI (October, 1960), 74–84.

Baritz, Loren. "The Historian as Playwright," *Nation,* Vol. CXCV (November 24, 1962), 340–43.

Barker, Charles A. "Needs and Opportunities in American Social and Intellectual History," *Pacific Historical Review,* Vol. XX (February, 1951), 1–10.

Barker, E. "Historian Too Must Stand Trial," *New York Times Magazine,* December 9, 1945, p. 9.

Bartlett, Richard A. "Of Librarians and Historians," *Journal of Library History,* Vol. I (April, 1966), 125–26.

Barzun, Jacques. "History as a Liberal Art," *Journal of the History of Ideas,* Vol. VI (January, 1945), 81–88.

Bauer, Richard H. "The Study of History," *Social Studies*, Vol. XXXIX (April, 1948), 150–58, 220–30, 267–72, 303–11.

Bastert, R. H. "The New American History and its Audience," *Yale Review*, Vol. XLVI, No. 2 (December, 1956), 245–59.

Baumer, Franklin L. "Intellectual History and Its Problems," *Journal of Modern History*, Vol. XXI (September, 1949), 191–203.

Beale, Howard K. "The Professional Historian: His Theory and His Practice," *Pacific Historical Review*, Vol. XXII (August, 1953), 227–55.

Beck, Lewis White. "The Limits of Skepticism in History," *South Atlantic Quarterly*, Vol. XLIX (October, 1950), 461–68.

Beckman, Alan C. "Hidden Themes in the Frontier Thesis: An Application of Psychoanalysis to Historiography," *Comparative Studies in Society and History*, Vol. VIII (April, 1966), 361–82.

Bemis, Samuel F. "American Foreign Policy and the Blessings of Liberty," *American Historical Review*, Vol. LXVII (January, 1962), 291–305.

———. "First Gun of a Revisionist Historiography for the Second World War," *Journal of Modern History*, Vol. XIX (March, 1947), 55–59.

Benison, Saul. "Reflections on Oral History," *American Archivist*, Vol. XXVII (January, 1965), 71–77.

Bennett, Edward. "History and Science," *Social Science*, Vol. XXVII (June, 1952), 132–37.

Berthoff, Rowland. "The American Social Order: A Conservative Hypothesis," *American Historical Review*, Vol. LXV (April, 1960), 495–514.

Bestor, Arthur. "History, Social Studies and Citizenship: The Responsibility of the Public Schools," American Philosophical Society *Proceedings*, Vol. CIV (1960), 549–57.

"Big Boom in History," *Newsweek*, Vol. XLIX (February 25, 1957), 113–14.

Bill, Shirley A. "The Really Crucial Matter: Proper Constitutional History," *Mid-America*, Vol. XLVIII (April, 1966), 126.

Billington, Ray A. "Why Some Historians Rarely Write History: A Case Study of Frederick Jackson Turner," *Mississippi Valley Historical Review*, Vol. L (June, 1963), 3–27.

Bingham, Woodbridge. "Historical Training and Military Intelligence," *Pacific Historical Review*, Vol. XV (June, 1946), 201–206.

Binkley, William C. "Two World Wars and American Historical Scholarship," *Mississippi Valley Historical Review*, Vol. XXXIII (June, 1946), 3–26.

Bock, Kenneth E. "Evolution and Historical Process," *American Anthropology*, Vol. LIV (October–December, 1952), 486–96.

Bonner, James C. "The Writing of History," *Georgia Review*, Vol. XIV (Fall, 1960), 334–45.

Bonner, Thomas N. "Civil War Historians and the 'Needless War,' " *Journal of the History of Ideas*, Vol. XVII (April, 1956), 193–216.

———. "Henry Adams: A Sketch and an Analysis," *Historian*, Vol. XX (November, 1957), 58–79.

Boyd, Julian P. "A Modest Proposal to Meet an Urgent Need," *American Historical Review*, Vol. LXX (January, 1965), 329–49.

Bridenbaugh, Carl. "The Great Mutation," *American Historical Review*, Vol. LXVIII (January, 1963), 315–31.

Brinton, Crane. "Many Mansions," *American Historical Review*, Vol. LXIX (January, 1964), 309–26.

———. "Something Went Wrong: Three Views of the Heritage of the Early 19th Century," *Journal of the History of Ideas*, Vol. XIV (June, 1953), 457–62.

———. "Toynbee's City of God," *Virginia Quarterly Review*, Vol. XXXII (Summer, 1956), 361–75.

Brown, Robert E. "Liberalism, Conservatism, and History," *Centennial Review*, Vol. VII (Summer, 1963), 317–26.

Bruun, Geoffrey. "Challenge and Response," *Saturday Review*, Vol. XLIV (May 27, 1961), 16–17.

Cairns, John C. "Carl Becker: An American Liberal," *Journal of Politics*, Vol. XVI (November, 1954), 623–44.

———. "Clio and the Queen's First Minister," *South Atlantic Quarterly*, Vol. LII (October, 1953), 505–20.

———. "The Historian in the Western World," *South Atlantic Quarterly*, Vol. LI (October, 1952), 504–14.

———. "The Successful Quest of Henry Adams," *South Atlantic Quarterly*, Vol. LVII (Spring, 1958), 168–93.

Carson, George Barr. "Changing Perspective in Soviet Historiography," *South Atlantic Quarterly*, Vol. XLVII (April, 1948), 186–95.

———. "The Proper Scope of History," *Western Humanities Review*, Vol. X (Winter, 1955–56), 37–44.

Cartwright, William H. "Clio, a Muse Bemused," *Indiana Magazine of History*, Vol. LIX (June, 1963), 121–34.

Caughey, John W. "Historians' Choice: Results of a Poll Recently Published on American History and Biography," *Mississippi Valley Historical Review*, Vol. XXXIX (September, 1952), 289–302.

————. "Our Chosen Destiny," *Journal of American History*, Vol. LII (September, 1965), 239–51.

Challener, Richard D., and Maurice Lee, Jr. "History and the Social Sciences," *American Historical Review*, Vol. LXI (January, 1956), 331–38.

Clough, Shepard B. "Economics and History," *Social Education*, Vol. XVI (January, 1950), 7–13.

Coates, William H. "Relativism and the Use of Hypothesis in History," *Journal of Modern History*, Vol. XXI (March, 1949), 23–27.

Cohn, Bernard S. "An Anthropologist Among the Historians," *South Atlantic Quarterly*, Vol. LXI (Winter, 1962), 13–28.

Cole, Wayne S. "American Entry into World War II: A Historiographical Appraisal," *Mississippi Valley Historical Review*, Vol. XLIII (March, 1957), 595–617.

Coleman, Peter J. "Beard, McDonald, and Economic Determinism in American Historiography—A Review Article," *Business Historical Review*, Vol. XXXIV (Spring, 1960), 113–21.

Colie, R. L. "Johan Huizinga and the Task of Cultural History," *American Historical Review*, Vol. LXIX (April, 1964), 607–30.

Colman, Gould P. "Oral History—An Appeal for More Systematic Procedures," *American Archivist*, Vol. XXVIII (January, 1965), 79–84.

Commager, Henry S. "The Search for a Usable Past," *American Heritage*, Vol. XVI (February, 1965), 4–9, 90–96.

————. "Should the Historian Make Moral Judgments," *American Heritage*, Vol. XVII (February, 1966), 26–27, 87–93.

Cook, Albert. "The Merit of Spengler," *Centennial Review*, Vol. VII (Summer, 1963), 306–16.

Cooke, W. Henry. "History and International Understanding," *Pacific Historical Review*, Vol. XV (September, 1946), 305–11.

Coulborn, Rushton. "Toynbee's Reconsiderations: A Commentary," *Journal of World History*, Vol. VIII (1964), 1–47.

Cowan, Thomas. "The Historian and the Philosophy of Science," *Isis*, Vol. XXXVIII (November, 1947), 11–18.

Craven, Avery O. "An Historical Adventure," *Journal of American History*, Vol. LI (June, 1964), 5–20.

Curti, Merle. "The Democratic Theme in American Historical Literature," *Mississippi Valley Historical Review*, Vol. XXXIX (June, 1952), 3–28.

———. "Intellectuals and Other People," *American Historical Review*, Vol. LX (January, 1955), 259–82.

Degler, Carl N. "The Sociologist as Historian: Riesman's *The Lonely Crowd*," *American Quarterly*, Vol. XV (Winter, 1963), 483–97.

De Novo, John A. "Edward Channing's 'Great Work' Twenty Years After," *Mississippi Valley Historical Review*, Vol. XXXIX (September, 1952), 257–74.

Destler, C. M. "Some Observations on Contemporary Historical Theory," *American Historical Review*, Vol. LV (April, 1950), 503–29.

De Voto, Bernard. "Easy Chair," *Harper's*, Vol. CXCVIII (April, 1949), 52–55.

Dixon, Elizabeth I. "The Implications of Oral History in Library History," *Journal of Library History*, Vol. I (January, 1966), 59.

Dodd, Wayne. "A New Look at Cultural History," *Bucknell Review*, Vol. XV (May, 1967), 26–40.

Donald, David. "American Historians and the Causes of the Civil War," *South Atlantic Quarterly*, Vol. LIX (Summer, 1960), 351–55.

Dorn, Walter L. "Personality and History: The Significance of the Individual in World Events," *Journal of Higher Education*, Vol. XXXIII (January, 1962), 20–29.

Dorpalen, Andreas. "Historiography as History: The Work of Gerhard Ritter," *Journal of Modern History*, Vol. XXXIV (March, 1962), 1–18.

Dozer, Donald M. "History as Force," *Pacific Historical Review*, Vol. XXXIV (November, 1965), 375–95.

Duberman, Martin. "The Limitations of History," *Antioch Review*, Vol. XXV (Summer, 1965), 283–96.

Dunne, Peter Masten. "The Renaissance and the Reformation: A Study in Objectivity (Legends Black and White)," *Pacific Historical Review*, Vol. XXVI (May, 1957), 107–22.

Eaton, Clement. "Recent Trends in the Writing of Southern History," *Louisiana Historical Quarterly*, Vol. XXXVIII (1955), 26–42.

Eisenstadt, A. S. "History Is Now," *Journal of Higher Education*, Vol. XXIX (October, 1958), 353–60, 408.

Ekirch, Arthur A., Jr. "Military History: A Civilian Caveat," *Military Affairs*, Vol. XXI (Summer, 1957), 49–54.

———. "Parrington and the Decline of American Liberalism," *American Quarterly*, Vol. III (Winter, 1951), 295–308.

Ellis, Elmer. "The Profession of Historian," *Mississippi Valley Historical Review*, Vol. XXXVIII (June, 1951), 3–20.

Esterquest, Frank L. "History Without Chronology or Geography," *Mississippi Valley Historical Review*, Vol. XXXIII (March, 1947), 629–45.

Feis, Herbert. "The Prankishness of History," *Virginia Quarterly Review*, Vol. XLI (Winter, 1965), 58–66.

Fellows, Erwin W. "Approaches to Experience: A Comparison of Science, Art, and History," *South Atlantic Quarterly*, Vol. LVI (Summer, 1957), 341–49.

Finer, Herman, "Acton as Historian and Political Scientist," *Journal of Politics*, Vol. X (November, 1948), 603–35.

Finkelstein, J. J. "Mesopotamian Historiography," American Philosophical Society *Proceedings*, Vol. CVII (1963), 461–72.

Finkelstein, Joseph. "Freshman History: The Neglected Course," *Liberal Education*, Vol. XLVI (May, 1960), 267–72.

Fogel, R. W. "The New Economic History," *Economic Historical Review*, Vol. XIX (December, 1966), 642-56.

Ford, Guy S. "Some Suggestions to American Historians," *American Historical Review*, Vol. XLIII (January, 1938), 253–69.

Fox, Edward Whiting. "History and Mr. Toynbee," *Virginia Quarterly Review*, Vol. XXXVI (Summer, 1960), 458–68.

Frankel, Charles. "Philosophy and History," *Political Science Quarterly*, Vol. LXXII (September, 1957), 350–69.

Galbraith, John S. "Some Reflections on the Profession of History," *Pacific Historical Review*, Vol. XXXV (February, 1966), 1–14.

Gall, Morris. "The Future of History," *Social Education*, Vol. XXIX (May, 1965), 269–71.

Galloway, B. P. "Economic Determinism in Reconstruction Historiography," *Southwestern Social Science Quarterly*, Vol. XLVI (December, 1965), 244–54.

Garraty, John A. "How to Write a Biography," *South Atlantic Quarterly*, Vol. LV (January, 1956), 73–86.

————. "The Interrelations of Psychology and Biography," *Psychological Bulletin*, Vol. LI (November, 1954), 569–82.

Gay, Peter. "Carl Becker's Heavenly City," *Political Science Quarterly*, Vol. LXXII (June, 1957), 182–99.

Gersehenkron, Alexander. "On the Concept of Continuity in History," American Philosophical Society *Proceedings*, Vol. CVI (June 29, 1962), 195–209.

Gershoy, Leo. "Carl Becker on Progress and Power," *American Historical Review*, Vol. LV (October, 1949), 22–35.

————. "Zagorin's Interpretation of Becker: Some Observations," *American Historical Review*, Vol. LXII (October, 1956), 12–17.

Gilb, Corinne L. "Should We Learn More About Ourselves," *American Historical Review*, Vol. LXVI (July, 1961), 987–93.

————. "Time and Change in Twentieth Century Thought," *Journal of World History*, Vol. IX (part 4, 1966), 867–80.

Glover, Richard. "War and Civilian Historians," *Journal of the History of Ideas*, Vol. XVIII (January, 1957), 84–100.

Gold, Milton. "In Search of a Historian," *Centennial Review*, Vol. VII (Summer, 1963), 282–305.

Goldman, Eric F. "Origins of Beard's *Economic Origins of the Constitution*," *Journal of the History of Ideas*, Vol. XIII (April, 1952), 234–49.

Goodykoontz, Colin B. "The Founding Fathers and Clio," *Pacific Historical Review*, Vol. XXIII (February, 1954), 111–24.

Gottschalk, Louis. "A Professor of History in a Quandary," *American Historical Review*, Vol. LIX (January, 1954), 273–86.

Gould, Clarence P. "History—A Science?" *Mississippi Valley Historical Review*, Vol. XXXII (December, 1945), 375–88.

Greene, Jack P. "The Flight from Determinism . . . Recent Literature on the . . . American Revolution," *South Atlantic Quarterly*, Vol. LXI (Spring, 1962), 235–59.

Greene, John C. "Objectives and Methods in Intellectual History," *Mississippi Valley Historical Review*, Vol. XLIV (June, 1957), 58–74.

Greene, Theodore M. "A Philosophical Appraisal of the Christian Interpretation of History," *Pacific Historical Review*, Vol. XXVI (May, 1957), 123–30.

Gressley, Gene M. "The Turner Thesis: A Problem in Historiography," *Agricultural History*, Vol. XXXII (October, 1958), 227–49.

Gundersheimer, W. L. "The Patterns of History," *Reporter*, Vol. XXXIV (April 21, 1966), 50–52.

Halle, Louis J. "Does History Have a Future?" *Saturday Review*, Vol. XLIII (April 23, 1960), 17–18, 56.

Handlin, Oscar. "The History in Men's Lives," *Virginia Quarterly Review*, Vol. XXX (Summer, 1954), 534–41.

Harbison, E. Harris. "The 'Meaning of History' and the Writing of History," *Church History*, Vol. XXI (1952), 97–107.

Harrison, J. A. "Time and the American Historian," *South Atlantic Quarterly*, Vol. LXIV (Summer, 1965), 362–66.

Harrison, Thomas S. "The Historian and Crisis," *Prairie Schooner*, Vol. XXV (1951), 166–78.

Hartz, Louis. "American Historiography and Comparative Analysis: Further Reflections," *Comparative Studies in Society and History*, Vol. V (July, 1963), 365–77.

Hayes, Carlton J. H. "The American Frontier—Frontier of What?" *American Historical Review*, Vol. LI (January, 1946), 199–216.

Helde, Thomas T. "Historians and Historical Knowledge," *Maryland Historical Magazine*, Vol. LIX (September, 1964), 243–61.

Helmer, Olaf, and Nicholas Rescher. "On the Epistemology of the Inexact Sciences," *Management Science*, Vol. VI (October, 1959), 25–52.

Herrick, Francis H. "The Profession of History," *Pacific Historical Review*, Vol. XXXI (February, 1962), 1–20.

Hicks, John D. "The Personal Factor in the Writing of History," *Pacific Northwest Quarterly*, Vol. LV (July, 1964), 97–104.

———. "What's Right with the History Profession," *Pacific Historical Review*, Vol. XXV (May, 1956), 111–25.

Higham, John. "American Intellectual History: A Critical Appraisal," *American Quarterly*, Vol. XIII (Summer, 1961), 219–33.

———. "Beyond Consensus: The Historian as Moral Critic," *American Historical Review*, Vol. LXVII (April, 1962), 609–25.

———. "The Cult of American Consensus: Homogenizing Our History," *Commentary*, Vol. XXVII (1959), 93–101.

———. "Intellectual History and Its Neighbors," *Journal of the History of Ideas*, Vol. XV (June, 1954), 339–47.

———. "The Rise of American Intellectual History," *American Historical Review*, Vol. LVI (April, 1951), 453–71.

"History as a Living Art," *Saturday Review of Literature*, Vol. XXXI (September 4, 1948), 20.

Hofstadter, Richard. "Beard and the Constitution: The History of an Idea," *American Quarterly*, Vol. II (Fall, 1950), 195–213.

―――. "Turner and the Frontier Myth," *American Scholar*, Vol. XVIII (Autumn, 1949), 433–43.

Holborn, Hajo. "Greek and Modern Concepts of History," *Journal of the History of Ideas*, Vol. X (January, 1949), 3–13.

―――. "History and the Humanities," *Journal of the History of Ideas*, Vol. IX (January, 1948), 65–69.

Hollingsworth, J. Rogers. "Consensus and Continuity in Recent American Historical Writing," *South Atlantic Quarterly*, Vol. LXI (Winter, 1962), 40–50.

Holt, W. Stull. "An Evaluation of the Report on Theory and Practice in Historical Study," *Pacific Historical Review*, Vol. XVIII (May, 1949), 233–42.

―――. "The Idea of Scientific History in America," *Journal of the History of Ideas*, Vol. I (June, 1940), 352–62.

Hoover, Dwight W. "Some Comments on Recent United States Historiography," *American Quarterly*, Vol. XVII (Summer, 1965), 299–318.

Hughes, H. Stuart. "The Historian and the Social Scientist," *American Historical Review*, Vol. LXVI (October, 1960), 20–46.

―――. "Is Contemporary History Real History?" *American Scholar*, Vol. XXXII (Autumn, 1963), 516–25.

Huston, James A. "Do Historians Seek the Truth," *Social Studies*, Vol. XLIV (November, 1953), 258–64.

Iggers, Georg G. "The Idea of Progress: A Critical Reassessment," *American Historical Review*, LXXI (October, 1965), 1–17.

―――. "The Idea of Progress in Recent Philosophies of History," *Journal of Modern History*, Vol. XXX (September, 1958), 215–26.

Jameson, J. F. "The Future Uses of History," *American Historical Review*, Vol. LXV (October, 1959), 61–71.

Jones, Howard M. "The Nature of Literary History," *Journal of the History of Ideas*, Vol. XXVIII (April–June, 1967), 147–60.

Jordan, Philip D. "The Usefulness of Useless Knowledge," *Historian*, Vol. XXII (May, 1960), 237–49.

Jordy, William. "Henry Adams and Francis Parkman," *American Quarterly*, Vol. III (Spring, 1951), 52–68.

Kellar, Herbert A. "The Historian and Life," *Mississippi Valley Historical Review*, Vol. XXXIV (June, 1947), 3–26.

Kennan, George F. "The Experience of Writing History," *Virginia Quarterly Review*, Vol. XXXVI (Spring, 1960), 205–14.

———. "History vs. Current Events," *School and Society*, Vol. LXXXIX (March 11, 1961), 102.

Kennedy, Thomas C. "Charles A. Beard and the 'Court Historians,' " *Historian*, Vol. XXV (August, 1963), 439–50.

Koch, Adrienne. "The Historian as Scholar," *Nation*, Vol. CXCV (November 24, 1962), 357–61.

Kohn, Hans. "A Historian's Creed for Our Time," *South Atlantic Quarterly*, Vol. LII (July, 1953), 341–48.

———. "Pondering the Past," *Saturday Review of Literature*, Vol. XXXIII (May 14, 1949), 24.

Krieger, Leonard. "The Horizons of History," *American Historical Review*, Vol. LXIII (October, 1957), 62–74.

———. "The Uses of Marx for History," *Political Science Quarterly*, Vol. LXXV (September, 1960), 255–78.

Kreiszewski, Charles. "The Pivot of History," *Foreign Affairs*, Vol. XXXII (April, 1954), 388–401.

Kristeller, Paul O. "The Philosophical Significance of the History of Thought," *Journal of the History of Ideas*, Vol. VII (June, 1946), 360–66.

Kroeber, A. L. "An Anthropologist Looks at History," *Pacific Historical Review*, Vol. XXVI (August, 1957), 281–87.

Krug, Mark M. "History and the Social Sciences: The Narrowing Gap," *Social Education*, Vol. XXIX (December, 1965), 515–20.

Lamb, W. Kaye. "The Archivist and the Historian," *American Historical Review*, Vol. LXVIII (January, 1963), 385–91.

Lampard, E. E. "American Historians and the Study of Urbanization," *American Historical Review*, Vol. LXVII (October, 1961), 49–61.

Langer, William L. "The Historian and the Present," *Vital Speeches*, Vol. XIX (March 1, 1953), 312–14.

———. "The Next Assignment," *American Historical Review*, Vol. LXIII (January, 1958), 283–304.

Laprade, W. T. "Obstacles in Studying History," *South Atlantic Quarterly*, Vol. LIX (Spring, 1960), 204–14.

Lasch, Christopher. "The Historian as Diplomat," *Nation*, Vol. CXCV (November 24, 1962), 348–53.

Latourette, K. S. "The Christian Understanding of History," *American Historical Review*, Vol. LIV (January, 1949), 259–76.

Lauch, A. R. "Is History a Science," *Western Humanities Review*, Vol. IX (Autumn, 1955), 349–58.

Lee, Dwight E., and R. N. Beck. "The Meaning of Historicism," *American Historical Review*, Vol. LIX (April, 1954), 568–77.

Lee, Everett S. "The Turner Thesis Re-examined," *American Quarterly*, Vol. XIII (Spring, 1961), 77–83.

Lehmberg, Stanford E. "The Divine Art and its Uses: Some Early English Views on the Utility of History," *Historian*, Vol. XX (November, 1957), 24–38.

Leontief, Wassily. "When Should History Be Written Backwards?" *Economic Historical Review*, Vol. XVI (August, 1963), 1–8.

Lerner, Robert E. "Turner and the Revolt Against E. A. Freeman," *Arizona and the West*, Vol. V (Summer, 1963), 101–108.

Levenson, Joseph R. "Redefinition of Ideas in Time," *Far East Quarterly*, Vol. XV (May, 1956), 399–404.

Link, Arthur S. "A Decade of Biographical Contributions to Recent American History," *Mississippi Valley Historical Review*, Vol. XXXIV (March, 1948), 637–52.

Loewenberg, Bert J. "Some Problems Raised by Historical Relativism," *Journal of Modern History*, Vol. XXI (March, 1949), 17–23.

Lord, Clifford L. "Localized History in the Age of Explosions," *North Carolina Historical Review*, Vol. XL (April, 1963), 221–31.

Lovejoy, Arthur O. "Historiography and Evaluation: A Disclaimer," *Journal of the History of Ideas*, Vol. X (January, 1949), 141–42.

———. "Reflections on the History of Ideas," *Journal of the History of Ideas*, Vol. I (January, 1940), 3–23.

McKelvey, Blake. "American Urban History Today," *American Historical Review*, Vol. LVII (July, 1952), 919–29.

McMahon, F. E. "The Meaning of History," *Commonweal*, Vol. LXVII (January 31, 1958), 454–57.

Mandel, Arthur A. "The Case for Economic History," *American Journal of Economics and Sociology*, Vol. X (October, 1950), 61–69.

Mandelbaum, Maurice. "Concerning Recent Trends in the Theory of Historiography," *Journal of the History of Ideas*, Vol. XVI (October, 1955), 506–17.

Mann, Golo. "How Not to Learn from History," *Yale Review*, Vol. XLI (March, 1952), 380–90.

Marcus, John T. "The Changing Consciousness of History," *South Atlantic Quarterly*, Vol. LX (Spring, 1961), 217–25.

———. "Time and the Sense of History: East and West," *Comparative Studies in Society and History*, Vol. III (January, 1961), 123–39.

Marks, Harry J. "Ground Under Our Feet: Beard's Relativism," *Journal of the History of Ideas*, Vol. XIV (October, 1953), 628–33.

Masur, Gerhard. "Distinctive Traits of Western Civilization: Through the Eyes of Western Historians," *American Historical Review*, Vol. LXVII (April, 1962), 591–608.

Matson, Floyd W. "History As Art: The Psychological-Romantic View," *Journal of the History of Ideas*, Vol. XVIII (April, 1957), 270–79.

Mattingly, Garrett. "The Historian of the Spanish Empire," *American Historical Review*, Vol. LIV (October, 1948), 32–48.

May, Henry F. "The Recovery of American Religious History," *American Historical Review*, Vol. LXX (October, 1964), 79–92.

———. "Shifting Perspectives on the 1920's," *Mississippi Valley Historical Review*, Vol. XLIII (December, 1956), 405–27.

Maynard, Theodore. "Muse and the Myth," *Catholic World*, Vol. CLXXXIII (July, 1956), 270–75.

Mead, Margaret. "Anthropologist and Historian: Their Common Problems," *American Quarterly*, Vol. III (Spring, 1951), 3–13.

Mead, Sidney. "Church History Explained," *Church History*, Vol. XXXII (March, 1963), 17–31.

Moceri, James. "Some Observations on Contemporary Historical Theory: Reply," *American Historical Review*, Vol. LVI (April, 1951), 760–66.

Morasky, Robert L. "The Case Method Approach to Teaching History," *Social Studies*, Vol. LVII (October, 1966), 199–204.

Morison, Samuel Eliot. "Faith of a Historian," *American Historical Review*, Vol. LVI (January, 1951), 261–75.

Morse, Richard M. "The Modern Scholar and the Americas," *Political Science Quarterly*, Vol. LXV (December, 1950), 522–37.

Morton, Louis. "The Historian and the Study of War," *Mississippi Valley Historical Review*, Vol. XLVIII (March, 1962), 599–613.

Mowry, George E. "The Uses of History by Recent Presidents," *Journal of American History*, Vol. LIII (June, 1966), 6–18.

Mullett, Charles F. "The Novelist Confronts Clio," *South Atlantic Quarterly*, Vol. LX (Winter, 1961), 56–70.

"Nationalism Is Not Enough," *Time*, Vol. XLIX (March 3, 1947), 76.

Neff, E. "On the Uses of History and the Abuses of Historians," *New Republic*, Vol. CXXIV (January 15, 1951), 28.

Neil, William M. "The Americans as Elite: An Essay in the Cultural Approach to History," *Indiana Magazine of History*, Vol. LVIII (March, 1961), 29–40.

Neilson, Francis. "Time and the Pattern of History," *American Journal of Economic Sociology*, Vol. XIII (October, 1953), 27–37.

Nevins, Allan. "Is History Made by Heroes," *Saturday Review*, Vol. XXXVIII (November 5, 1955), 9–10.

———. "Not Capulets, Not Montagues," *American Historical Review*, Vol. LXV (January, 1960), 253–70.

Nichols, Roy F. "Adaptation versus Invention as Elements in Historical Analysis," American Philosophical Society *Proceedings*, Vol. CVIII (October 20, 1964), 404–10.

———. "History in a Self-governing Culture," *American Historical Review*, Vol. LXXII (January, 1967), 411–24.

———. "Kansas Historiography: The Technique of Cultural Analysis," *American Quarterly*, Vol. IX (Spring, 1957), 85–91.

———. "Postwar Reorientation of Historical Thinking," *American Historical Review*, Vol. LIV (October, 1948), 78–89.

"Niebuhr on History," *Time*, Vol. LIII (May 2, 1949), 68.

Nixon, H. C. "Paths to the Past: The Presidential Addresses of the Southern Historical Association," *Journal of Southern History*, Vol. XVI (February, 1950), 33–39.

Nowell, Charles E. "Has the Past a Place in History," *Journal of Modern History*, Vol. XXIV (December, 1952), 331–40.

Nulle, S. H. "History and Class," *Western Humanities Review*, Vol. IX (Winter, 1954–55), 65–74.

Pargellis, Stanley. "Clio in a Strait Jacket," *American Quarterly*, Vol. XI (Summer, 1959), 225–31.

Parker, Harold T. "A Tentative Reflection on the Inter-Disciplinary Approach and the Historian," *South Atlantic Quarterly*, Vol. LVI (January, 1957), 105–11.

Partin, Robert. "The Use of History," *Alabama Review*, Vol. XIX (April, 1966), 109–24.

Pearce, Roy Harvey. "Note on Method in the History of Ideas," *Journal of the History of Ideas*, Vol. IX (June, 1948), 372–79.

Perkins, Dexter. "American Wars and Critical Historians," *Yale Review*, Vol. XL (Summer, 1951), 682–95.

————. "We Shall Gladly Teach," *American Historical Review*, Vol. LXII (January, 1957), 291–309.

Pessen, Edward. "Can Historians Be Objective?" *Bulletin* of the Association of American Colleges, Vol. XLI (May, 1955), 316–27.

Peterson, E. N. "Historical Scholarship and World Unity," *Social Research*, Vol. XXVII (January, 1961), 439–50.

Posony, Stefan T., and Dale O. Smith. "The Utility of Military History," *Military Affairs*, Vol. XXII (Winter, 1958, 1959), 216–18.

Potter, David M. "An Appraisal of Fifteen Years of the Journal of Southern History," *Journal of Southern History*, Vol. XVI (February, 1950), 25–32.

————. "The Historian's Use of Nationalism and Vice Versa," *American Historical Review*, Vol. LXVII (July, 1962), 924–50.

Ralph, P. L. "Toynbee and the Human Spirit," *Saturday Review*, Vol. XXXIX (September 1, 1956), 18–19.

Randall, J. G. "Historianship," *American Historical Review*, Vol. LVIII (January, 1953), 249–64.

Read, Conyers. "The Social Responsibilities of the Historian," *American Historical Review*, Vol. LV (January, 1950), 275–85.

Redlich, Fritz. "Toward Comparative Historiography," *Kyklos*, Vol. XI, No. 3 (1958), 362–89.

Reynolds, Beatrice. "Shifting Currents in Historical Criticism," *Journal of the History of Ideas*, Vol. XIV (October, 1953), 471–92.

Rodabaugh, James H. "Historical Societies: Their Magazines and Their Editors," *Wisconsin Magazine of History*, Vol. XLV (Winter, 1961–62), 115–23.

Roszak, Theodore. "The Historian as Psychiatrist," *Nation*, Vol. CXCV (November 24, 1962), 343–48.

Rubin, Louis D., Jr. "The Historical Image of Modern Southern Writing," *Journal of Southern History*, Vol. XXII (May, 1956), 147–66.

Ruchames, Louis. "The Historian as Special Pleader," *Nation*, Vol. CXCV (November 24, 1962), 353–57.

Rundell, Walter, Jr. "History Teaching: A Legitimate Concern," *Social Education*, Vol. XXIX (December, 1965), 521–24, 528.

Savelle, Max. "The Function of History in the Age of Science," *Historian*, Vol. XXII (August, 1960), pp. 347–60.

————. "Historian's Progress, or, The Quest for Sancta Sophia," *Pacific Historical Review*, Vol. XXVII (February, 1958), 1–26.

————. "The Philosophy of the General: Toynbee Versus the Naturalists," *Pacific Historical Review*, Vol. XXV (February, 1956), 55–67.

Schlesinger, Arthur M. "An American Historian Looks at Science and Technology," *Isis*, Vol. XXXVI (October, 1946), 162–66.

Schlesinger, Arthur M., Jr. "The Historian as Artist," *Atlantic*, Vol. CCXII (July, 1963), 35–41.

———. "On the Inscrutability of History," *Encounter*, Vol. XXVII (November, 1966), 10–17.

———. "On the Writing of Contemporary History," *Atlantic*, Vol. CCXIX (March, 1967), 69–74.

———. "The Thread of History: Freedom or Fatality," *Reporter*, Vol. XIII (December 15, 1955), 45–47.

Schmitt, Bernadotte E. "With How Little Wisdom," *American Historical Review*, Vol. LXVI (January, 1961), 299–322.

Schmitt, Hans A. "Perspective: A Note on Historical Judgments," *South Atlantic Quarterly*, Vol. LXII (Winter, 1963), 57–66.

Schoenwald, Richard L. "Historians and the Challenge of Freud," *Western Humanities Review*, Vol. X (Spring, 1956), 99–108.

Schuyler, Robert L. "Contingency in History," *Political Science Quarterly*, Vol. LXXIV (September, 1959), 321–33.

———. "The Historical Spirit Incarnate: Frederic William Maitland," *American Historical Review*, Vol. LVII (January, 1952), 303–22.

———. "Man's Greatest Illusion," American Philosophical Society *Proceedings*, Vol. XCII (1948), 46–51.

Sellen, Robert W. "Theodore Roosevelt: Historian with a Moral," *Mid-America*, Vol. XLI (October, 1959), 223–40.

Sellers, Charles Grier, Jr. "Andrew Jackson versus the Historians," *Mississippi Valley Historical Review*, Vol. XLIV (June, 1958), 615–34.

Sellers, James L. "Before We Were Members—The Mississippi Valley Historical Association," *Mississippi Valley Historical Review*, Vol. XL (June, 1953), 3–24.

Shafer, Boyd C. "The Historian in America," *Southwest Historical Quarterly*, Vol. LX (January, 1957), 381–86.

———. "History, Not Art, Not Science, but History: Meanings and Uses of History," *Pacific Historical Review*, Vol. XXIX (May, 1960), 159–70.

———. "Men Are More Alike," *American Historical Review*, Vol. LVII (April, 1952), 593–612.

———. "The Study of History in the United States," American Association of University Professors *Bulletin*, Vol. L (September, 1964), 232–40.

Sharabi, H. B. "The Existential Approach to History," *Historian*, Vol. XXVI (February, 1964), 167–75.

Shyrock, R. H. "American Historiography: A Critical Analysis and a Program," American Philosophical Society *Proceedings*, Vol. CXXXVII (1943), 35–46.

Simons, William E. "The Study of History and the Military Leader," *Military Affairs*, Vol. XXVI (Spring, 1962), 22–27.

Simonson, Harold P. "Frederick Jackson Turner: Frontier History as Art," *Antioch Review*, Vol. XXIV (Summer, 1964), 201–11.

Simpson, Lesley Byrd. "Thirty Years of the Review," *Hispanic American Historical Review*, Vol. XXIX (May, 1949), 188–204.

Skotheim, Robert A. "Environmental Interpretations of Ideas by Beard, Parrington, and Curti," *Pacific Historical Review*, Vol. XXXIII (February, 1964), 35–44.

———. "The Writing of American Histories of Ideas: Two Traditions in the XXth Century," *Journal of the History of Ideas*, Vol. XXV (April–June, 1964), 257–78.

Smith, Bradford. "Biographer's Creed," *William and Mary Quarterly*, Vol. XX (April, 1953), 190–95.

Smith, Harrison. "The World and Professor Toynbee," *Saturday Review*, Vol. XXXVII (December 11, 1954), 24.

Smith, Lacey Baldwin. "A Study of Textbooks on European History During the Last Fifty Years," *Journal of Modern History*, Vol. XXIII (September, 1951), 250–56.

Solt, Leo F. "Some Reflections upon the Study of English History," *Social Studies*, Vol. XLVIII (March, 1957), 75–80.

Sorenson, Lloyd R. "Charles A. Beard and German Historiographical Thought," *Mississippi Valley Historical Review*, Vol. XLII (September, 1955), 274–97.

———. "Historical Currents in America," *American Quarterly*, Vol. VII (Fall, 1955), 234–46.

Speiser, E. A. "The Ancient Near East and Modern Philosophies of History," American Philosophical Society *Proceedings*, Vol. XLV (1951), 583–88.

Stampp, Kenneth M. "The Historian and Southern Negro Slavery," *American Historical Review*, Vol. LVII (April, 1952), 613–24.

Stearns, Raymond P. "College History and its New Approaches," *School and Society*, Vol. LXXXII (August 20, 1955), 49–55.

Stephenson, Wendell H. "A Quarter Century of American Historiography," *Mississippi Valley Historical Review*, Vol. XLV (June, 1958), 3–22.

———. "William P. Trent as a Historian of the South," *Journal of Southern History*, Vol. XV (May, 1949), 151–77.

Stevens, Harry R. "Contemporary American Biographical Writing: Trends and Problems," *South Atlantic Quarterly*, Vol. LV (July, 1956), 359–70.

Steward, Julian H. "Cultural Causality and Law," *American Anthropologist*, Vol. LI (January–March, 1949), 1–27.

Strayer, J. R. "To Preserve the Past," *Saturday Review of Literature*, Vol. XXXIV (March 17, 1951), 14.

Strong, E. W. "Theories of History," *Journal of Modern History*, Vol. XXXIII (March, 1961), 50–52.

Strout, Cushing. "Causation and the American Civil War," *History and Theory*, Vol. I, No. 2 (1961), 175–85.

———. "Historical Thought in America," *Virginia Quarterly Review*, Vol. XXVIII (April, 1952), 242–57.

———. "The Unfinished Arch: William James and the Idea of History," *American Quarterly*, Vol. XIII (Winter, 1961), 505–15.

Sullivan, Richard E. "Clio in the Classroom," *Centennial Review*, Vol. VII (Summer, 1963), 353–74.

———. "Toynbee's Debtors," *South Atlantic Quarterly*, Vol. LVIII (Winter, 1959), 77–90.

Susman, Warren I. "History and the American Intellectual: Uses of a Usable Past," *American Quarterly*, Vol. XVI (Summer, 1964), 243–63.

Swift, Donald C., and Rodney F. Allen. "History Instruction and Human Aspirations: A Proposed Synthesis," *Social Studies*, Vol. LVII (January, 1966), 3–7.

Swing, Raymond. "Is History Bunk?" *Saturday Review of Literature*, Vol. XXXIII (June 3, 1950), 6–7, 38–40.

Taylor, George V. "History, Literature, and the Public at Large," *North Carolina Historical Review*, Vol. XLII (April, 1965), 180–91.

Thaden, Edward C. "Encounters with Soviet Historians," *Historian*, Vol. XX (November, 1957), 80–95.

Tholfsen, Trygve. "What Is Living in Croce's Theory of History," *Historian*, Vol. XXIII (May, 1961), 283–302.

Thompson, Paul van K. "Hope, History, and Hysteria," *Catholic World*, Vol. CLXXVI (December, 1952), 176–83.

Thorndike, Lynn. "Whatever Was, *Was* Right," *American Historical Review*, Vol. LXI (January, 1956), 265–83.

Tinder, Glenn. "The Necessity of Historicism," *American Political Science Quarterly*, Vol. LV (September, 1961), 560–65.

Tuchman, Barbara W. "History by the Ounce," *Harper's*, Vol. CCXXXI (July, 1965), 65–68.

Unger, Irwin. "The 'New Left' and American History: Some Recent Trends in United States Historiography," *American Historical Review*, Vol. LXXII (July, 1967), 1211–36.

Usher, A. P. "The Significance of Modern Empiricism for History and Economics," *Journal of Economic History*, Vol. IX (November, 1949), 137–55.

Van Alstyne, Richard W. "History and the Imagination," *Pacific Historical Review*, Vol. XXXIII (February, 1964), 1–24.

Van Nostrand, John J. "The Historian as Teacher," *Pacific Historical Review*, Vol. XXI (February, 1952), 111–20.

Von Laue, T. H. "Is There a Crisis in the Writing of History?" *Bucknell Review*, Vol. XLV (December, 1966), 1–15.

Wallace, Elisabeth. "Goldwin Smith on History," *Journal of Modern History*, Vol. XXVI (September, 1954), 220–32.

Watson, Richard L., Jr. "American Political History," *South Atlantic Quarterly*, Vol. LIV (January, 1955), 107–26.

Webb, Walter P. "The Historical Seminar: Its Outer Shell and Its Inner Spirit," *Mississippi Valley Historical Review*, Vol. XLII (June, 1955), 3–23.

———. "History as High Adventure," *American Historical Review*, Vol. LXIV (January, 1959), 265–81.

Wecter, Dixon. "History and How to Write It," *American Heritage*, Vol. VIII (August, 1957), 24–27.

Weisberger, Bernard A. "The Dark and Bloody Ground of Reconstruction Historiography," *Journal of Southern History*, Vol. XXV (November, 1959), 427–47.

Wellemeyer, J. F., Jr. "Survey of United States Historians, 1952, and a Forecast," *American Historical Review*, Vol. LXI (January, 1956), 339–52.

Welter, Rush. "The History of Ideas in America: An Essay in Redefinition," *Journal of American History*, Vol. LI (March, 1965), 599–614.

Wendon, John. "Christianity, History, and Mr. Toynbee," *Journal of Religion*, Vol. XXXVI (July, 1956), 139–49.

White, Hayden V. "The Abiding Relevance of Croce's Idea of History," *Journal of Modern History*, Vol. XXXV (June, 1963), 109–24.

White, Lynn, Jr. "The Changing Past," *Harper's*, Vol. CCIX (November, 1954), 29–34.

———. "The Social Responsibility of Scholarship: History. Is Clio a Tutelary Muse?" *Journal of Higher Education*, Vol. XXXII (October, 1961), 357–61.

White, Morton G. "The Revolt Against Formalism in American Social Thought of the Twentieth Century," *Journal of the History of Ideas*, Vol. VIII (April, 1947), 131–52.

Wiener, Philip P. "The Logical Significance of the History of Thought," *Journal of the History of Ideas*, Vol. VII (June, 1946), 366–73.

Wildman, John H. "Lord Acton's Approach to History," *South Atlantic Quarterly*, Vol. XLVII (April, 1948), 196–203.

Wilkins, Burleigh T. "Frederick York Powell and Charles A. Beard: A Study in Anglo-American Historiography and Social Thought," *American Quarterly*, Vol. XI (Spring, 1959), 21–39.

———. "Pragmatism as a Theory of Historical Knowledge: John Dewey on the Nature of Historical Inquiry," *American Historical Review*, Vol. LXIV (July, 1959), 878–90.

Williams, Jay. "History and Historical Novels," *American Scholar*, Vol. XXVI (Winter, 1956–57), 67–74.

Williams, L. P. "History and the Current Irrationalism," *Education*, Vol. LXXIII (February, 1953), 371–73.

Williams, W. A. "The Age of Re-forming History," *Nation*, CLXXXII (June 30, 1956), 552–54.

———. "Fire in the Ashes of Scientific History," *William and Mary Quarterly*, Vol. XIX (April, 1962), 274–87.

———. "A Note on Charles Austin Beard's Search for a General Theory of Causation," *American Historical Review*, Vol. LXII (October, 1956), 59–80.

Wilson, Tyson. "The Case for Military History and Research," *Military Affairs*, Vol XXI (Summer, 1957), 54–60.

Wish, Harvey. "The American Historian and the New Conservatism," *South Atlantic Quarterly*, Vol. LXV (Spring, 1966), 178–91.

Wolfe, Bertram D. "Dissecting Opinion on Toynbee," *American Mercury*, Vol. LXIV (June, 1947), 748–56.

————. "Operation Rewrite: Agony of Soviet Historians," *Foreign Affairs*, Vol. XXXI (October, 1952), 39–57.

Woodward, C. Vann. "The Age of Reinterpretation," *American Historical Review*, Vol. LXVI (October, 1960), 1–19.

Zagorin, Perez. "Carl Becker on History. Prof. Becker's Two Histories: A Skeptical Fallacy," *American Historical Review*, Vol. LXII (October, 1956), 1–11.

Index

Acton, Lord: 50, 53
Adams, Brooks: 26, 58
Adams, Henry: 16, 19, 58, 144; and Darwinism, 83–84
Adler, Mortimer: 53
Alexander the Great: 71
Anderson, Sherwood: 72
ARCADIA conference: 88
Athens, Greece: 113
Augustine, Saint: 26, 100
Auschwitz, Poland: 56
Austria: 81
Aydelotte, William O.: 134

Bailey, Thomas A.: 40f.
Bancroft, George: 51; and idea of progress, 53
Barnes, Harry Elmer: 48
Barth, Karl: 4
Bassett, John S.: 12
Bastille, the: 86
Bauer, Richard: 36
Beard, Charles A.: 14, 114, 131; and economic interpretation of Constitution, 42; as a relativist, 59, 133
Beck, Lewis: on relativism, 135–36
Becker, Carl: 48, 114f., 131; as a relativist, 59
Behaviorism: 4
Bennett, Edward: 44
Benson, Lee: 78, 136
Berlin, Isaiah: 80
Bestor, Arthur: 40, 91, 144; on determinism, 66–67
Billington, Ray: 134
Bonaparte, Napoleon: 30, 71, 79, 86, 89, 121
Bossuet, Bishop: 26
Bourbons, the: 89
Bowditch, John: 26
Bridenbaugh, Carl: on individual in history, 62

Brinton, Crane: 25, 36, 92; and lessons of history, 41; on history as art, 138
Bryan, William Jennings: 45
Buchenwald, East Germany: 56
Bury, J. B.: 93–94
Butterfield, Herbert: 27

Cairns, John: 76
Camus, Albert: 4, 113
Carlyle, Thomas: 113
Carr, E. H.: 5
Carson, George B.: 52, 74
Causation, historical: pluralism in, 76–80; underlying and immediate factors in, 86; see also history
Chamberlain, Neville: 23
Channing, Edward: 95
Charles XII: 92
Churchill, Winston S.: 88f.
Cochran, Thomas C.: 73
Cole, Wayne S.: 128
Confederacy, the : 89
Conquest of Mexico, The: 124
Conquest of Peru, The: 124
Cortes, Hernán: 113
Cotterill, Robert S.: on continuity in history, 85
Craven, Avery: on generalization in history, 49–50
Cuba: 89

Dante: 38
Darwin, Charles: 120, 142
Darwinism: 83, 84, 93, 142
Davidson, Philip: 64
Dawson, Christopher: 27
Destler, Chester M.: 42; on relativism, 135
De Voto, Bernard: 34, 123
Diet of Worms: 81
Dodd, William E.: 12

Dovring, Folke: 73; on contingency in history, 94–95
Dreiser, Theodore: 8
Duberman, Martin: 43, 73

Einstein, Albert: 120, 128
Eisenstadt, A. S.: 15, 34
Elba, island of: 79
Eliot, T. S.: 16, 38
England: 42, 88, 90
Enlightenment, the: 87, 133; historians of, 93
Existentialism: 4, 112, 115

Filler, Louis: 8
Finley, M. I.: 48
Ford, Guy S.: 32
Fort Sumter: 66
France: 25, 86, 88; *ancien régime* of, 66
Frankel, Charles: 61
Freud, Sigmund: 72, 94, 126

Garraty, John: 78
Germany: 57, 81, 88ff.
Gettysburg, battle of: 121
Gibbon, Edward: 93, 135
Gilbert, Felix: 38
Glaab, Charles N.: 49
Gold, Milton: 132
Goodykoontz, Colin: 27–28
Gottschalk, Louis: 49, 96; on individual in history, 63
Grant, Ulysses S.: 89
Greene, John C.: 6, 35
Guicciardini, Francesco: 93

Handlin, Oscar: 68
Hapsburgs, the: 89
Harbison, E. Harris: 27
Harrison, Thomas S.: 17
Hayes, Carlton J. H.: 14; on continuity in history, 85
Hayes, Rutherford B.: 92
Hays, Samuel P.: 70
Hegel, Georg F. W.: 98
Hegelianism: 93
Herder, Johann Gottfried: 69
Herodotus: 121
Hexter, J. H.: 28, 128, 142; and narrative history, 34; and historical re-examination, 37; and anti-presentism, 43
Hicks, John D.: 41, 123, 138
Higham, John: on historian as moralist,

52–53; on multiple causation in history, 78
Historian and History, The: 12
Historians: and intellectual history, 8–9; relativist school of, 13; and society, 15; and causation, 18–19; and presentism, 25; as moralists, 50–53; literary, 57; and anti-determinism, 65–66; and personality, 69–72; Marxist, 86; and acceptance of bias, 115–16; subjectivity of, 116–17, 136–37; and intuition, 117–20; and similarity to scientists, 120; and the human condition, 125–26; need for balance in, 127–28
Historicism: 13; German school of, 83
Historiography: as mirror of age, 9–10; main currents of, 15; Christian school of, 27, 34, 100f., 133; ancient, 47, 133; scientific school of, 47, 57–58, 83, 93; Roman, 100; romantic school of, 124–25; *see also* history
History: intellectual, 5–7; scientific school of, 12; and the social sciences, 14; dangers in lessons of, 22–24; and faith, 27–28; as a narrative, 28, 33–35; and perspective, 29–30, 43–47; and historical facts, 36; and presentism, 37–43; generalization in, 47–50; laws in, 58; and irrationality, 72–73; inevitability in, 80–81; motivation in, 82; continuity in, 84–90; change in, 90–92; universal, 99; and the human condition, 113–14; and imagination, 120–22; as literature, 122–24; definition of, 132; Chinese idea of, 133; uniqueness of, 139; and memory, 140–41; evolutionary character of, 141–43; *see also* historians, historiography
Hitler, Adolph: 21, 23, 30, 45, 71, 89
Hofstadter, Richard: 14, 73
Hoover, Dwight: 43
Hoover, Herbert: 45
Hughes, H. Stuart: 13, 28; on historical causation, 82
Huizinga, Johan: 120
Hume, David: 93

Interpretation of History: 119

Jameson, J. Franklin: 84
Johns Hopkins University: 57
Jordan, Philip D.: 139

Kennan, George F.: 122; on causation in history, 76–77
Kohn, Hans: 42, 68
Krey, August C.: 70
Krieger, Leonard: 7, 81

Langer, William L.: 29, 72
Laprade, W. T.: 41
Lee, Robert E.: 79, 121
Lenin (Vladimir Ilich Ulyanov): 140
Lord, Clifford: 46
Louis XIV: 25, 71
Lovejoy, Arthur O.: 7, 17
Luther, Martin: 79, 81

McCarthyism: 79
Machiavelli, Niccolò: 93
McIlwain, C. H.: 24, 25, 52
McKinley, William: 45
McNeill, William H.: 96
Malin, James C.: 63, 139
Marcus, John T.: 36
Maritain, Jacques: 38
Marx, Karl: 26, 98
Marxism: 93
Mass society: 56–57
Mattingly, Garrett: 67, 144
Mead, Sidney: 82, 143
Metahistory: definition of, 98; see also Toynbee, Arnold J.
Mexico City, Mexico: 89
Middle Ages: and providential history, 92–93
Mommsen, Theodor: 135
Montcalm, Marquis de: 124
Montesquieu, Charles de Secondat, baron de: 87
Morison, Samuel Eliot: 35–36, 121; on historian as moralist, 51–52; on need for balance, 127–28
Morse, R. M.: 63
Motley, John L.: 124
Munich, conference at: 23

Namier, Lewis: 41
Neo-orthodoxy: 4, 122
Netherlands, the: 124
Nevins, Allan: 77, 125, 137
New Deal: 12
"New History": 48; major tenets of, 59
Nichols, Roy F.: 14, 19, 28, 49, 134; and historical perspective, 46–47; on contingency in history, 94

Niebuhr, Reinhold: 4, 27, 122
Noble, David: 51
North Africa: 88
Nye, Russel B.: 138

O'Neill, Eugene: 72
Orosius: 100

Parkman, Francis: 5; on reasons for French defeat, 47–48; and idea of progress, 53
Parrington, Vernon L.: 12
Partin, Robert: 52
Pirenne, Henri: and importance of Islam, 42
Pope, Alexander: 63
Potter, David: 74
Prescott, William H.: 113, 124
Prince, The: 93
Progress, idea of: 13, 53
Puritans, the: 51

Randall, J. H., Jr.: 6
Randall, John G.: 129
Ratner, Sidney: 72
Read, Conyers: 39, 49
Reformation, the: 79, 86
Relativism: 84, 112, 131; in history, 59–60; principles of, 114–15; attack on scientific history by, 132–33; defects of, 134–35
Renaissance, the: 93
Revolution, French: 17, 79, 113, 140; causes of, 86–88
Rise of the Dutch Republic, The: 124
Robespierre, Maximilien de: 86
Robinson, Edward Arlington: 16
Robinson, James Harvey: 48, 58
Romanticism: 57
Rome: fall of, 17, 79; time of troubles in, 100; empire of, 135
Roosevelt, Franklin D.: 45
Roosevelt, Theodore: 81
Rousseau, Jean-Jacques: 87

Sanders, Jennings: 63–64
Sartre, Jean-Paul: 4
Savelle, Max: 36, 67; on multiple causation in history, 77–78
Saveth, Edward N.: 115
Schlatter, Richard: 49
Schlesinger, Arthur M., Jr.: 96, 118, 137; on role of individual in history, 65

Schmitt, Hans: 129
Schoenwald, Richard L.: 126
Schuyler, Robert L.: on multiple causation in history, 77
Sellers, Charles G.: 12, 143
Sellers, James L.: 44
Serbia: 81
Shafer, Boyd: 24, 25, 29, 30; and function of history, 46
Shakespeare, William: 53
Shyrock, Richard: 112
Simonson, Harold P.: 119
Smith, Bradford: 67
Smith, Henry Nash: 73
Smith, Lacey Baldwin: 26
Smith, Page: 12, 22, 67, 72; and presentism, 38
Smyth, Howard M.: 66
Social Science Research Council *Bulletin* 64: 63
Socrates: 38
Solon: 92
Solt, Leo: 43
Somervell, D. C.: 99
Somme (river): 89
Sorenson, Lloyd: 71
South, the: 45
Soviet Union, the: 23, 76; kulaks in, 56
Spain: 124
Spengler, Oswald: 18
Stalin, Joseph: 30
Stearns, Raymond P.: 43
Stephenson, Wendell: 144
Strout, Cushing: 78, 80, 90–91
Study of History, A: 13, 27, 98ff.; *see also* Toynbee, Arnold J.
Sullivan, Richard E.: 38, 65
Sumeria: 25
Swing, Raymond Gram: 76

Taylor, A. M.: 58
Teggart, Frederick J.: 19–20
Tennis Court Oath: 86
Tenochtitlán: 113

Tholfsen, Trygve: 68, 69, 78
Thucydides: 5, 21, 33, 53, 113
Tigner, Hugh S.: 17
Tilbury Town: 16
Tillich, Paul: 4, 119
Tolstoy, Leo: 53
Toynbee, Arnold J.: 5, 13, 27, 65; historical theories of, 98–100
Tuchman, Barbara: 35
Turner, Frederick Jackson: 119

United States, the: 23, 89, 90
Usher, Abbott P.: 94

Van Alstyne, Richard: 91, 122
Van Nostrand, John J.: 30, 36
Veracruz, Mexico: 89
Vico, Giambattista: 26
Voltaire: 87, 93
Von Laue, T. H.: 27; on function of history, 54

Wars: World War I, 3, 18–19, 40, 79; British experience in, 89; Meuse-Argonne front in, 89; Peloponnesian, 5; World War II, 16, 18, 40, 56, 86, 112, 125; debate over strategy in, 88–90; American Civil, 28, 78, 79, 89; Mexican, 89
Wasteland, The: 16
Weimar, republic of: 45
Weisinger, Herbert: 116
Weiss, Paul: 61
Wells, H. G.: 18, 100
Welter, Rush: 6
White, Lynn, Jr.: 118
White, William Allen: 8
Willcox, W. B.: 71–72, 96
Williams, William A.: 72
Wish, Harvey: 78, 137
Wolfe, James: 124
Woodward, C. Vann: 35, 74

Zola, Emile: 137